BREAK FREE WITH BOOKKEEPING

Life on Your Terms

by

Bill Rogers & DeAnna Rogers

Break Free with Bookkeeping
Life on Your Terms
By Bill Rogers and DeAnna Rogers

Copyright © 2025

ISBN: 979-8-9911866-8-1 (Paperback)
ISBN: 979-8-9911866-9-8 (eBook)

Printed in the United States of America
First Edition, 2025

Publisher:
Empower Growth Academy

Email: info@stayathomebookkeeper.com
Website: www.stayathomebookkeeper.com

Disclaimer: The information contained in this book is for educational and informational purposes only. The author and publisher have made every effort to ensure the accuracy of the information herein. However, the information is provided without warranty, either express or implied. The author and publisher shall not be liable for any losses or damages incurred as a result of applying the information in this book.

Free Resources and Tools

SCAN ME

https://stayathomebookkeeper.co/resource

Table of Contents

Break Free, Live on Your Terms

Have you ever caught yourself staring at the ceiling at night, asking: *"Is this really it? Is this the life I'm meant to live?"*

For some, the question comes in a corporate cubicle under fluorescent lights, somewhere between the third Zoom call of the morning and the twenty unread emails waiting for a response. For others, it comes while folding laundry at midnight, kids finally asleep, wishing you had something to call your own—something that gave you both purpose and financial freedom. For retirees, it sneaks in quietly as they calculate the numbers one more time, hoping the retirement check will cover not just bills, but the life they actually want to live. And for many, it comes in the form of a deep sigh, a weary recognition that they're simply *burned out.*

That's the grind.

And here's the truth: it's not your fault.

The grind was built into the system most of us were taught to trust. Go to school. Get a degree. Get a good job. Work hard, climb the ladder, and eventually—hopefully—retire with enough to enjoy the good years. That's the promise we were sold.

But promises like that rarely come true anymore.

The Struggles We All Share

Life looks different for everyone, but the frustrations, fears, and pressures are strikingly similar. Let's take a closer look.

The Corporate Cage

Corporate employees live by calendars that aren't their own. Someone else tells them where to be, when to show up, what deadlines matter, and how their performance will be measured. It doesn't matter if you're the hardest-working person in the room—your pay is capped, your freedom is limited, and your time is not your own.

Promotions rarely solve the problem. More money often comes with more stress, longer hours, and even less flexibility. And the so-called "stability" of a corporate job can disappear overnight with a layoff, merger, or restructuring. One decision in a boardroom can wipe out decades of loyalty.

The corporate grind whispers a painful truth: *you don't own your future here.*

The Mom Juggle

For moms, the grind has a different face. It looks like soccer practice schedules, grocery lists, meal prep, piles of laundry, school projects, and the quiet weight of wanting to do more without taking away from the people who need you most.

Motherhood is a calling and a privilege—but for many moms, it also comes with a nagging question: *"What about me?"*

What about the dream of contributing financially in a way that matters? What about building an identity beyond carpool and kitchen duty? What about showing your kids not just what sacrifice looks like, but what freedom and ownership can look like too?

The grind whispers to moms: *you don't get to have both—you have to choose.*

The Retiree's Reality

Retirement was supposed to be the prize at the end of the game. Work hard for forty years, save diligently, and then coast into a life of leisure. That's the picture many retirees had in mind.

But reality looks different.

Inflation eats away at fixed incomes. Health care costs rise. Savings don't stretch as far as planned. And after the initial joy of "no alarm clock," many retirees face long days wondering how to fill the hours. The desire for purpose doesn't retire when you do.

Retirees face a double grind: the financial grind of making ends meet, and the emotional grind of needing something meaningful to pour their energy into.

The grind whispers to retirees: *your best years are behind you.*

The Burnout Epidemic

Then there's the rest of us—people working long hours in schools, hospitals, restaurants, retail stores, or small businesses. The details differ, but the symptoms are the same:

- Chronic stress that doesn't go away after a weekend.

- Emotional exhaustion that makes you question if anything you do matters.

- A paycheck that never seems to keep up with effort.

- The gnawing suspicion that you're building someone else's dream while your own slips further away.

Burnout doesn't just steal energy. It steals joy. It leaves people feeling undervalued, unseen, and used up.

The grind whispers to burned-out workers: *this is as good as it gets.*

The Emotional Toll of the Grind

When you add it all up, the grind takes more than money. It takes:

- **Time.** Hours spent on commutes, overtime, and obligations you didn't choose.

- **Energy.** Exhaustion that bleeds into family life, leaving little left to give.

- **Confidence.** The quiet erosion of self-belief after years of playing small or being overlooked.

- **Hope.** The sneaky lie that life will never be different, so you might as well settle.

And yet—there's something powerful about the moment when you realize you've had enough. That moment is the turning point.

The Turning Point: Enough Is Enough

Every person who chooses a new path eventually hits a wall.

Maybe it's a corporate employee who realizes another promotion won't buy them freedom. Maybe it's a mom who looks at her kids and decides she wants them to see her not just as a caregiver, but as an example of possibility. Maybe it's a retiree who runs the numbers one more time and knows they need a way to supplement income. Or maybe it's a burned-out worker who simply can't stand another day of dragging themselves into a job they hate.

The turning point can feel scary. Change always does. But it's also liberating. Because once you admit to yourself, *"I want more,"* you've already taken the first step toward freedom.

Why Bookkeeping? Why Now?

So why bookkeeping?

Because it's the **hidden gem** nobody tells you about.

- Every business needs it.

- It's low-risk to start, with minimal upfront costs.

- You don't need a CPA license—just the right training.

- You can start small and scale as big as you want.

- It works whether you're a mom with a few hours a day, a corporate escapee wanting to match your salary, or a retiree looking for both purpose and income.

Bookkeeping is not about staring at spreadsheets all day—it's about building a life of freedom. It's about owning your time, your income, and your choices.

Stories of Freedom

Throughout this book, you'll hear about people who were just like you.

- A mom who started with one client and now earns more than her old salary—while being home for every milestone.

- A corporate manager who left the boardroom behind and built a six-figure agency in under two years.

- A retiree who supplements their pension with a bookkeeping practice, working 15 hours a week from the comfort of home.

- A burned-out worker who discovered that their organizational skills translated perfectly into a business they now own and love.

These aren't fairy tales. They're proof that bookkeeping is a path to freedom.

What You'll Gain from This Book

This book is more than a "how-to." It's a blueprint for living life on your terms. Inside, you'll discover:

- How to shift your mindset from employee to entrepreneur.

- The exact steps to set up your bookkeeping business legally and financially.

- How to choose and use the right tools, like QuickBooks Online and AI.

- How to brand yourself so clients see you as the trusted professional they need.

- How to find and win clients without begging or chasing.

- How to build systems so your business runs smoothly without consuming your life.

- How to scale, if you choose, into a six-figure business or beyond.

- How to design work that fits around your life—not the other way around.

Your Invitation

If you've read this far, chances are the grind has already taken more from you than you want to admit. Maybe it's time. Time to stop waiting. Time to stop wondering. Time to step into something new.

This book isn't just about bookkeeping. It's about **breaking free**. It's about reclaiming your time, your confidence, and your future.

So take a deep breath. Turn the page.

Your journey to *Break Free with Bookkeeping: Life on Your Terms* starts now.

Chapter 1

Breaking Free from the Grind

The Weight of the Everyday Grind

You know that feeling when the alarm rings before dawn and you lie there for a moment, already tired, already thinking about everything waiting for you?

That's the grind.

The grind steals your mornings, your peace, and eventually, your belief that life could be different. It's what happens when the rhythm of surviving drowns out the possibility of thriving.

It's not laziness or lack of ambition that keeps people stuck—it's momentum. We get swept into a system that rewards busyness and applauds exhaustion, a world that measures worth in hours worked and boxes checked. Somewhere along the way, we start believing that trading time for a paycheck is the only respectable way to live.

But deep down, you know something isn't right. You feel it every Sunday night when anxiety creeps in about Monday morning. You feel it every time you look at your schedule and realize your own life isn't on it anywhere.

If that sounds familiar, you're not broken. You're waking up.

The Corporate Cage: Trading Time for Dollars

Corporate life sells a promise: stability, structure, and success. On paper it looks great—health benefits, paid vacation, maybe even a bonus if the numbers land just right. But behind the polished mission statements and HR slogans, the reality is often far less glamorous.

You wake up before the sun. You sit in traffic or stare into a glowing screen all day, juggling deadlines and meetings that multiply faster than you can clear them. You eat lunch at your desk. You check your phone at night "just to stay caught up." You give your best energy away before you ever get to use it for yourself.

It's easy to convince yourself it's fine—*everyone* does this. But quietly, something in you starts to ache. You begin to crave air, space, control.

Erica's Story

Erica spent fifteen years in middle management at a logistics firm. On paper, she was winning—corner office, six-figure salary, company car. Inside, she was drained. Her days started at six and rarely ended before nine. One night her eight-year-old slipped a note under her office door that said, *"Mom, are you coming to dinner?"* That note hit harder than any performance review ever could.

The next morning, sitting in traffic, Erica whispered out loud, "There has to be another way."

That whisper changed everything.

Two years later, she left corporate life. She started a small bookkeeping business from her home office, first part-time, then full-time. The salary came back. Her freedom did too. "The money's great," she says, "but what I love most is being at my own table for dinner."

Erica didn't quit because she couldn't handle corporate pressure; she left because she finally realized she wanted to own her *time*.

The Illusion of Security

People often stay in the corporate cage because it feels safe. The paycheck arrives every two weeks; the insurance card works when you need it. But security built on someone else's decision isn't security—it's dependency.

One reorganization meeting can change everything. You can give decades of loyalty to a company that can replace you with an email.

You don't need to hate your job to outgrow it. You just have to love your life enough to want more control over it.

The Mom Juggle: Too Much to Do, Not Enough Flexibility

Motherhood adds another layer to the grind—a beautiful, exhausting, emotional layer.

The days start early, end late, and blur together. There's breakfast to make, backpacks to pack, laundry that somehow multiplies overnight. Add a part-time job or a side gig, and you're stretched thinner than you ever thought possible.

Moms are the masters of multitasking, the unsung project managers of the world. But even superheroes have limits.

The Guilt Cycle

Ask any mom and she'll tell you about the guilt.

- Guilt for not earning enough.

- Guilt for wanting a career.

- Guilt for missing a moment.

- Guilt for dreaming of something that's hers alone.

Society tells mothers they can "have it all," then quietly judges them for trying. The truth is, what most moms want isn't everything—it's balance. They want to contribute financially *and* be present for their families. They want to work without guilt and rest without fear.

Melissa's Story

Melissa had three kids under ten and a husband who traveled for work. Most days felt like a marathon that never ended. She wanted to help financially but couldn't stomach the idea of punching a clock and paying for daycare just to watch most of her paycheck vanish.

A friend mentioned bookkeeping. Melissa laughed at first. "Numbers? That's not me." But curiosity got the better of her. She learned the basics online, took on one client, and discovered she *was* good with numbers— because she'd been managing a household budget like a CFO for years.

Three years later, Melissa runs a thriving bookkeeping business from home. She works around her kids' school schedules and vacations. "I don't feel guilty anymore," she says. "My kids see me working, but they also see me *there*—and that matters."

Why Moms Are Natural Entrepreneurs

Moms already possess the traits that make great business owners:

- Organization. Keeping a family running is a masterclass in systems and efficiency.

- Communication. From teachers to spouses, moms negotiate daily.

- Problem-solving. Every spilled cup and missed bus has trained them to adapt fast.

- Resilience. Motherhood builds grit like nothing else.

The difference is that entrepreneurship lets moms use those same skills on their own terms—and get paid what they're worth for it.

The Hidden Cost of "Doing It All"

A recent study by the American Psychological Association found that 70 percent of working mothers report feeling chronically overwhelmed. Most aren't tired because they can't handle life—they're tired because they've been told they must handle *everything*.

When the culture glorifies burnout as proof of commitment, rest starts to feel like failure. That's not balance—it's bondage.

The truth? You don't owe anyone proof that you can do it all. You deserve work that gives as much as it takes.

Small Moments of Clarity

Sometimes awareness sneaks up quietly. It's that drive home after school drop-off when you think, *"If I had two quiet hours, I could build something."* It's seeing another mom post about her small business and wondering, *"Could I?"*

The answer is yes—you could. You just need the right path.

And that path might look nothing like the one you expected.

The Retiree's Reality – More Years, Less Security

Retirement used to sound like freedom: mornings without alarms, afternoons of golf or grandkids, time finally reclaimed.

But modern retirement looks different. Costs rise, markets dip, and "fixed income" feels anything but fixed.

Many retirees discover a subtle panic beneath the calm. You've worked a lifetime, yet there's still that small voice asking, *"Will it be enough?"* And beyond the math, there's the question of meaning. After years of being needed, productive, relied upon, what happens when the phone stops ringing?

Harold knows that feeling.

Harold's Second Act

At 62 he retired from a logistics company. The first month felt like vacation; the second felt like limbo. "I went from managing fifty people to managing the TV remote," he jokes. The truth was, he missed purpose. When his neighbor mentioned she needed help organizing receipts for her small landscaping business, Harold offered to take a look. He learned QuickBooks in a weekend, cleaned up her books, and felt something he hadn't felt in years – relevance.

Within six months, he had three clients. At 68, Harold now earns a comfortable side income working about fifteen hours a week from home. "It's not about money," he says. "It's about waking up with a reason again."

Retirement doesn't have to mean the end of contribution. It can be the beginning of freedom on your terms – where experience meets flexibility.

The Burnout Epidemic

If you feel exhausted, you're not alone. A recent Gallup poll found that more than 60 percent of workers report feeling emotionally detached from their jobs, and nearly half describe themselves as chronically burned out.

Burnout isn't laziness. It's depletion. It's the natural outcome of a culture that glorifies overwork and under-rest. It's showing up, day after day, knowing you're capable of more but trapped in a system that won't let you breathe.

Tanya's Turnaround

Tanya worked in healthcare for two decades. She loved helping people, but the twelve-hour shifts, night calls, and constant staffing shortages were breaking her down. After one especially long weekend, she caught herself crying in the parking lot, unable to walk back inside. "I realized I couldn't keep saving everyone else while losing myself," she says.

A friend told her about bookkeeping. Skeptical but desperate, Tanya took a short online course. She landed her first client – a local chiropractor – and felt something shift. "I still help people," she says, "but now I do it in peace. I get to decide how much I give and when."

Burnout fades when ownership begins. That's the quiet truth no one tells you.

The Emotional and Mental Toll

The grind drains more than time; it drains identity. When you're constantly meeting expectations that aren't your own, you forget what your own even are. You stop dreaming because dreaming feels dangerous.

- Anxiety shows up as a constant buzz you can't turn off.

- Depression whispers, *"Why bother?"*

- Resentment creeps in – toward jobs, bosses, even loved ones.

- Confidence erodes until "I can't" feels safer than "I can."

But here's the thing – the very fatigue that scares you is also evidence of life. It means there's still a spark left. It means you still care. And caring can be rebuilt into something beautiful when you point it in the right direction.

The Moment of Clarity

Everyone who breaks free remembers the moment.

Sometimes it's dramatic – a layoff, a diagnosis, a missed childhood event that hurts too much to repeat. Other times it's subtle – a quiet afternoon when you realize you've been living on autopilot.

For most people, it starts as a whisper: *"I want more."*

That whisper is sacred. It's the first sign that you're ready for change. You don't have to know the whole plan yet; you just have to stop silencing that voice.

Linda's Lightbulb Moment

Linda was a project coordinator who spent her days color-coding spreadsheets for someone else's goals. One evening she closed her laptop and thought, "If I can manage million-dollar budgets for this company, why can't I manage books for businesses of my own?" That single question led her to research bookkeeping that night. Eighteen months later she had replaced her salary and replaced anxiety with autonomy.

Freedom always begins with one brave question.

Overcoming Fear and Doubt

Change invites fear. That's normal. Fear says, *"What if it doesn't work?"*

But try asking, *"What if it does?"*

Every person who has ever started something new has wrestled with the same doubts:

- *What if I fail?*

- *What if I look foolish?*

- *What if I'm not qualified?*

Yet the greatest risk isn't failure – it's regret. It's looking back five years from now wishing you'd tried.

Fear loses power when you move anyway. Momentum replaces anxiety with confidence. You don't have to leap – you just have to step.

Why Breaking Free Matters

Breaking free isn't rebellion; it's reclamation. It's taking back ownership of:

- Time – to decide when your day starts and ends.

- Choice – to work where, how, and with whom you choose.

- Security – to know your income comes from your effort, not someone else's whim.

- Purpose – to build something that reflects who you are, not what's on your badge.

When you control your time, everything changes: your health, your relationships, even the way you breathe.

The Hidden Path Forward

If these stories sound familiar – if you see yourself in the corporate cage, the mom juggle, the retiree's restlessness, or the quiet ache of burnout – then you already know why something has to change.

What you may not know is *how*.

The good news is, the path exists. It's not complicated, not reserved for the lucky or the wealthy. It's practical, learnable, and available to anyone ready to start.

That path is bookkeeping.

Bookkeeping isn't about spreadsheets – it's about stability. It's about using everyday skills – organization, communication, detail, trust – to build a business that gives you back the one thing you can't earn anywhere else: freedom.

In the next chapter, we'll pull back the curtain on why bookkeeping is the hidden gem of home-based business – a career that fits into *your* life instead of forcing your life to fit around it.

Because the goal isn't just to escape the grind. The goal is to live on your terms.

Chapter 1 Summary

- The grind takes many forms – corporate, family, retirement, burnout – but its cost is always the same: your freedom.

- Every story of change begins with a whisper: *"There has to be more than this."*

- Fear will always be present, but it doesn't get to make the decisions anymore.

- The first step to breaking free is realizing that your current story isn't the final draft.

Now turn the page. Chapter 2 reveals the opportunity hiding in plain sight – the simple, flexible, profitable business that ordinary people are using to reclaim their lives.

Why Bookkeeping is the Hidden Gem

The Hidden Door to Freedom

S ometimes the best opportunities don't shout.

They sit quietly in plain sight while the world runs past them chasing something louder.

That's bookkeeping.

It isn't the dream career anyone talked about at career day. No one said, *"I want to reconcile bank accounts when I grow up."*

And yet, for thousands of people who were exhausted, underpaid, or out of options, bookkeeping became the doorway to a completely different life.

You've probably met a bookkeeper before without realizing it. She might have been the woman at your networking group who always seemed calm while everyone else complained about deadlines. Or the retiree who mysteriously travels half the year yet never seems to worry about money. They're not lottery winners. They're bookkeepers.

Bookkeeping is simple, honest work that happens behind the scenes— but it's the foundation of every business that exists. Every transaction, every paycheck, every profit margin flows through the hands of someone who keeps the books.

What most people don't realize is this: those hands can be *yours.*

The Opportunity No One Talks About

The Reality of the Market

Small business is booming. In the U.S. alone, more than 5 million new businesses were registered last year—an all-time record. Most of them are small, owner-operated, and desperate for help managing their finances.

Those entrepreneurs don't need an accountant in a suit. They need a reliable person who can organize their QuickBooks, keep track of receipts, and make sure nothing falls through the cracks.

That's the modern bookkeeper.

Someone who blends trust with technology.

Someone who gives business owners the peace of mind that their numbers finally make sense.

During economic booms, businesses grow—and need bookkeepers to track the growth.

During downturns, businesses tighten budgets—but bookkeeping remains non-negotiable.

When COVID-19 forced millions to work from home, virtual bookkeeping didn't just survive; it exploded. Remote tools like QuickBooks Online, Xero, and Gusto turned what was once an office job into a laptop career.

That's why bookkeeping is one of the few industries that's *economy-proof.*

Money keeps moving, and someone has to keep score.

What Makes Bookkeeping Different

Most "work-from-home" ideas rely on hustle and hype—selling products, chasing algorithms, or talking strangers into buying things they don't need.

Bookkeeping is the opposite.

It's a professional service built on skill, not sales.

Once you learn it, your value is measurable and steady.

Businesses rely on you every month, which means recurring income instead of starting from zero each week.

There are no trending fads to chase, no inventory to stock, no late-night cold calls.

Just clear, consistent work that clients truly appreciate.

And unlike many traditional professions, bookkeeping grows with you.

You can start with one client and stay small, or build an agency with a team of bookkeepers under your brand. You decide how far to take it.

What Bookkeepers Actually Do

Let's strip away the mystery.

Here's what real-world bookkeeping looks like:

1. Record and Categorize Transactions

Every business has money flowing in and out. The bookkeeper's job is to make sure each transaction is recorded correctly—income, expenses, assets, liabilities. Modern software does most of the math; you just ensure it's accurate and labeled.

2. Reconcile Bank Accounts

Think of reconciliation as "balancing the checkbook," but digital. Each month, you compare bank statements to the books and verify that every dollar lines up. When it doesn't, you investigate and fix it. (That detective work is oddly satisfying.)

3. Generate Reports

You'll produce simple reports—Profit & Loss, Balance Sheet, Cash Flow—that help owners see where they stand. For many clients, these reports are eye-opening; they finally *understand* their business.

4. Collaborate with Accountants and Owners

Bookkeepers and accountants are teammates. You maintain the day-to-day data; accountants use that data for tax filing and strategy. Business owners lean on you for clarity throughout the year.

5. Streamline Systems

A modern bookkeeper is part technician, part organizer. You'll connect bank feeds, automate invoices, and tidy digital chaos. When your client sees their dashboard finally make sense, they'll call you a lifesaver—and mean it.

That's it. No calculus, no CPA exams. Just organization, accuracy, and communication.

A Peek Inside a Typical Day

Let's make it real.

Morning: Coffee, laptop, login. You start with a client dashboard. Maybe you manage the books for a small landscaping company and a local boutique. You check for new transactions, reconcile yesterday's deposits, and flag two questions for the owner.

Late Morning: A short Zoom with another client—an online coach— reviewing her monthly Profit & Loss. She admits, "I finally understand where my money's going." You smile, because that's the best part: clarity changes lives.

Afternoon: You write two invoices, send them through QuickBooks, and schedule automatic reminders. You finish the day knowing exactly what's complete. No commute. No meetings that could've been emails.

It's productive, peaceful work. A rhythm that fits around your life instead of swallowing it.

Who You Serve

You'll never run out of clients because every field needs books:

- Home-service companies (plumbers, landscapers, painters)
- Retail shops and boutiques
- E-commerce sellers
- Health and wellness professionals (chiropractors, coaches, gyms)
- Consultants and freelancers

Each one needs help with the same thing: keeping accurate records.

You're not selling luxury—you're providing necessity.

What You Can Earn

Bookkeeping isn't minimum-wage work. It's skilled, repeatable, and valuable.

Independent bookkeepers commonly charge $60 – $120 per hour, depending on experience and niche. Many shift quickly to monthly packages—$400 to $1,500 per client—creating reliable recurring revenue.

Here's a simple picture:

Clients	Average Fee	Monthly Income	Annual Income
3	$750	$2,250	$27,000
6	$1,000	$6,000	$72,000
10	$1,200	$12,000	$144,000

You choose your numbers. Want part-time flexibility? Three clients is plenty. Want to scale? Add more.

No glass ceilings. No performance reviews. Just possibility.

Stories of Transformation

Every bookkeeper begins with a story—a moment when they realize they've had the skills all along.

1. Maya – From Marketing Manager to Freedom Founder

Maya's career looked solid. A decade in marketing, good salary, nice office view. Yet every Sunday she felt that knot in her stomach—the dread of another week spent chasing numbers that weren't hers.

When layoffs hit, Maya took a severance package and a deep breath. She wanted something stable but flexible, professional but personal. She stumbled on bookkeeping through a podcast and laughed out loud. *Me? Numbers?*

Still, she tried. She learned QuickBooks Online, joined a few business groups, and offered to help a local landscaper clean up his books. By the third month he was referring her to his friends.

Two years later, Maya earns more than she did in corporate—working from a sunlit corner of her living room. She meets her clients on Zoom, wears jeans instead of blazers, and spends afternoons with her kids. "I don't just manage budgets anymore," she says. "I manage my life."

2. Jen – The Mom Who Reclaimed Herself

When Jen left her HR job after her second baby, she promised it was temporary. "Just until the kids are in school," she said. But the years rolled by and the gap on her résumé grew wider.

She tried side gigs—selling crafts, tutoring—but nothing stuck. She wanted something real, something she could build.

A friend mentioned bookkeeping. Jen took an online workshop and realized she'd been running her family like a business for years—tracking budgets, organizing schedules, solving problems on the fly. Within six months she had two clients; within a year she was making $4,000 a month.

But the money wasn't the only thing that changed. "I stopped introducing myself as 'just a mom,'" she says. "Now my kids watch me run a business. They see what's possible."

3. Ron – The Retiree Who Found a New Mission

After twenty years in the Air Force, Ron wasn't built for idle days. Retirement left him restless. When his daughter asked him to help her salon track expenses, he opened QuickBooks and fell in love with the order of it.

"I realized bookkeeping was like maintenance," he says. "Keep the systems running, and everything else works."

Now, in his late 60s, Ron manages books for five small businesses. He works mornings, golfs in the afternoons, and teaches other veterans to start their own firms. "It's purpose without pressure," he says. "And that's freedom."

Freedom by Design

Bookkeeping doesn't give you freedom by accident—it gives you a framework to *design* it.

Imagine this week:

- Monday: You reconcile two clients before noon, then spend the afternoon volunteering at your child's school.

- Tuesday: You start late, enjoy breakfast with your spouse, and finish invoices by three.

- Wednesday: You work from a café by the lake because the Wi-Fi's good and the view is better.

- Thursday: You knock out payroll for a gym owner who texts, "You saved me again!"

- Friday: You close your laptop before lunch and head into the weekend free from guilt or backlog.

That's not fantasy. That's an average week for thousands of bookkeepers who realized they could earn income without sacrificing life.

You decide your hours. You decide your workload. You decide who you serve.

That's real ownership.

The Confidence Shift

When people start their first bookkeeping business, they expect to learn software.

What surprises them most isn't QuickBooks—it's themselves.

Running your own business rewires how you think. The first time a client thanks you sincerely for "making sense of the chaos," you feel it: *I'm capable.*

The first time you quote your price and the client says "Yes," you realize your time has value.

The first time you take a Tuesday off just because you can, you understand the phrase "life on your terms."

Confidence isn't built by reading motivational quotes; it's built by keeping promises to yourself. Every small win—every invoice sent, every report delivered—is proof that you can create results.

Bookkeeping teaches responsibility, independence, and trust. But above all, it teaches belief.

What Makes Bookkeepers Indispensable

You might wonder, *"If software can do so much, why do businesses still need people?"*

Because numbers don't interpret themselves.

A report can show income down 10 percent, but it takes a human to ask, *why?*

Automation can record expenses, but it can't reassure a stressed business owner at midnight.

That's where you come in. You're not just data entry; you're a partner in clarity.

You make people feel safe with their money—and that's priceless.

Scaling Your Freedom

One of the quiet joys of bookkeeping is scalability.

You can stay solo forever or build a small team.

- Some bookkeepers specialize in niches—real estate, health, construction—charging premium rates.

- Others hire assistants or junior bookkeepers to handle recurring tasks.

- Some even create digital courses or consulting packages teaching other owners financial literacy.

You can expand income without expanding stress. The systems you build once continue to serve you.

The Numbers Behind the Freedom (Expanded)

Let's zoom out and picture real scenarios.

Scenario A – The Part-Timer

Three steady clients at $600 each per month = $1,800.

Workload: about 8–10 hours weekly.

Perfect for retirees or parents wanting supplemental income.

Scenario B – The Balanced Builder

Six clients averaging $900 each = $5,400 monthly.

Workload: roughly 20 hours a week.

This level replaces many full-time salaries while keeping half your week free.

Scenario C – The Agency Owner

Ten clients at $1,200 each = $12,000 monthly, $144,000 a year.

You might hire a virtual assistant or subcontractor.

Still fully remote, still yours.

Every level is achievable with the same foundation you'll learn in this book.

You control the volume; the volume no longer controls you.

Why Bookkeeping Feels So Fulfilling

People assume fulfillment comes from passion projects, but true satisfaction often comes from usefulness.

Bookkeeping gives instant feedback. You help real people run real businesses better. You see relief on their faces when numbers finally make sense. You become the calm in someone else's storm.

And that feeling—the mix of competence and gratitude—never gets old.

The Bridge Between Safety and Freedom

Most careers force you to choose: stability or autonomy.

Bookkeeping gives you both.

It's safe because the need never disappears.

It's free because you decide the structure.

That combination is rare—and powerful.

You don't have to burn bridges to corporate life or abandon security to chase dreams. You can start this business gradually, one client at a time, while you still work elsewhere. The bridge is wide and steady.

Reframing the Skill You Already Have

Take a moment and consider everything you already know how to do:

- Stay organized under pressure.
- Communicate clearly.
- Solve problems quickly.
- Keep commitments.

Those aren't soft skills. They're *business assets.*

Bookkeeping simply channels them into income.

Most of the women and men succeeding in this field didn't start with accounting degrees; they started with a decision to learn.

A Final Story – The Day Everything Changed for Clara

Clara worked in hospitality for fifteen years. When the pandemic hit, her hotel closed. Unemployment checks kept the lights on but crushed her spirit. One afternoon she scrolled past a post about virtual bookkeeping.

She almost ignored it. "I'm not a math person," she thought.

But something in her paused. She used QuickBooks free training account and spent the weekend exploring. Within a month she enrolled in training. Within six months she had her first paying client—a local bakery.

The day that bakery owner handed her a check and said, "You've made my life easier," Clara cried in her car. "I felt useful again," she says. "I felt *free*."

Today, she earns $80 K a year from her home office, often with a candle burning and jazz playing softly. "It's calm," she says. "After fifteen years of chaos, I built calm—and it pays me."

Your Next Step

You now see why bookkeeping is the hidden gem:

- It's practical.

- It's profitable.

- It's possible for anyone willing to learn.

The next step is turning possibility into structure.

In Chapter 3 – Laying the Foundation, we'll walk through:

- How to shift your mindset from employee to entrepreneur.

- How to set up the legal and financial basics.

- The simple tools that keep your business running.

- The first actions that attract clients and build confidence.

You've looked through the door. Now it's time to step through it.

Your story—the next success story someone else will read—is about to begin.

Additional resources, case studies, forms, and more are waiting for you at https://stayathomebookkeeper.co/resource. Visit the site now and enjoy a huge collection of resources that are absolutely free!

Chapter 3

Laying the Foundation

The Shift from Dreaming to Doing

You've made it this far for a reason.

Something in you knows it's time.

Maybe you've been thinking about leaving your job for months.

Maybe you've whispered to yourself that you want more freedom, more purpose, more control. You've read stories that sounded familiar—people who didn't have a plan at first but took a step anyway.

Now it's your turn.

This chapter isn't about theory or dreams anymore.

This is about *doing*.

It's where you start turning that whisper into a blueprint.

The truth is, starting a business isn't complicated—it's emotional. It's not the paperwork that stops people; it's fear. Fear of making mistakes, fear of not being "qualified," fear of the unknown.

But here's what I want you to remember before we dive in: you already have everything you need to begin.

You don't need a business degree or a perfect plan. You just need willingness and direction. The rest comes one step at a time.

The Mindset Shift: From Employee to Entrepreneur

For most of your life, you've probably worked *for* someone.

You were given schedules, deadlines, and paychecks.

You knew what was expected—and what would happen if you didn't deliver.

Being your own boss flips that script.

There's no one checking in, no annual review, no guaranteed paycheck every two weeks. That can feel terrifying—or it can feel thrilling. The difference is mindset.

Entrepreneurs think differently. They see opportunity instead of obstacles. They understand that mistakes aren't failures—they're feedback. They stop waiting for permission.

Ownership Thinking

When you work for yourself, you become the CEO of *you*.

That means:

- You set the tone for your day.

- You decide what "success" looks like.

- You take responsibility for results—good or bad.

It's both freedom and responsibility, but once you feel the rhythm of it, there's nothing more empowering.

Jessica's Story: Stepping Into Ownership

Jessica was a former teacher turned bookkeeper. For years she lived by bells and lesson plans. When she started her bookkeeping business, she panicked. "There's no principal to tell me what to do," she said.

Then one morning she wrote on a sticky note: *I am the boss now.* She stuck it on her laptop, and everything changed. She created her own routine, her own deadlines, her own rewards. Within six months she'd replaced her salary.

Jessica didn't become more skilled overnight—she just started thinking like an owner instead of an employee.

Designing Your Vision and Lifestyle Goals

When you start your bookkeeping business, you're not just building a job—you're designing a lifestyle.

Before you even open QuickBooks or pick a name, pause and ask yourself:

"What do I want my life to look like?"

Because this business should serve your life, not consume it.

Defining "Life on Your Terms"

Write down your answers to these three questions:

1. Income: How much money do I want to make each month?

2. Time: How many hours do I want to work each week?

3. Purpose: Why do I want this business? What will it give me that my current situation doesn't?

When you answer those honestly, you start to see the outline of your dream. Maybe it's working 20 hours a week and earning $5 000 a month. Maybe it's replacing a six-figure salary while working from home. Maybe it's simply never missing another family dinner.

The magic is that bookkeeping can fit *all* of those. You build it to fit you.

Vision in Action

Picture this:

You start your day with coffee instead of traffic. You work from a cozy office corner, your favorite playlist humming in the background. You take a mid-morning walk, then jump on a client call that feels more like collaboration than work.

You're still working hard—but it's for *you*.

That's the "life on your terms" you're creating right now.

Building the Skills You Need

You might be wondering, *"Okay, but what do I actually need to know?"*

The truth is simple: you don't have to know everything about accounting to start a successful bookkeeping business.

You just need enough knowledge to do excellent work, communicate clearly, and stay organized.

Bookkeeping Basics

At its core, bookkeeping is the process of tracking money—keeping a clear, organized record of where it comes from and where it goes.

Think about your own finances. Ever looked at your bank account and thought, *"Where did all my money go this month?"* Maybe it was too many Target runs or a few quiet subscription increases. Without tracking, you're guessing.

Bookkeeping removes the guesswork. It brings order to the chaos and clarity to the confusion.

You don't need a finance degree to do it. Bookkeeping isn't advanced accounting; it's practical financial organization. Once you learn the structure, it repeats across every business.

Why Bookkeeping Matters

Every business has money coming in and money going out.

- **Income:** payments from customers or clients

- **Expenses:** rent, payroll, supplies, software, or equipment

If no one tracks those movements, the owner never truly knows if they're profitable or quietly losing money.

Bookkeeping solves that problem—it organizes every transaction into proper categories, revealing exactly where the money is going and why.

With solid books, business owners can answer critical questions:

- Are we charging enough?

- Where are we overspending?

- Which products or clients are most profitable?

As a bookkeeper, you deliver peace of mind. You turn uncertainty into clarity—and that's priceless.

The Grocery Analogy

If you can go grocery shopping and put everything away, you can learn bookkeeping.

Your "groceries" are transactions; your "pantry, fridge, and freezer" are categories like rent, payroll, or supplies.

Put the ice cream in the pantry and you've got a mess—organization is your superpower.

A Quick Example

A client buys pens for the office. Where does that go?

Answer: Office Supplies.

Now they print new flyers. Where does that go?

Answer: Advertising Expense.

Once you see how transactions fit into categories, bookkeeping becomes a structured, repeatable rhythm.

The Bookkeeping Process

Bookkeeping follows a consistent rhythm of **reviewing, categorizing, reconciling, and reporting.**

Once your systems are in place, the work becomes efficient and predictable.

Daily & Weekly Work

- Connect your client's bank and credit-card accounts to QuickBooks Online.

- Categorize new transactions regularly—don't leave them sitting in the bank feed.

- Stay consistent; it keeps month-end fast and accurate.

Month-End Close

At the end of each month, you'll reconcile accounts—matching your records to the bank statement—then produce two key reports:

- **Profit & Loss Statement** (shows revenue and expenses)

- **Balance Sheet** (shows what the business owns and owes)

Quarterly Tasks

- Review financial reports for trends or inconsistencies.

- Confirm taxes such as sales or payroll filings are current.

- Help clients prepare for estimated tax payments.

Year-End Tasks

- Review accounts for accuracy and completeness.

- Reconcile outstanding items and corrections.

- Generate year-end statements for the CPA or tax preparer.

Bookkeeping is steady, repeatable, and deeply rewarding once you master its rhythm.

It's not about math—it's about clarity, consistency, and care.

QuickBooks Online (QBO)

Think of QBO as your main hub—the place where every client's financial activity lives.

You'll use it to:

- Connect bank accounts and credit cards

- Record and categorize transactions

- Generate reports and invoices

- Manage expenses

QuickBooks automates the heavy lifting so you can focus on accuracy and insight. The more you use it, the more intuitive it feels. Whether you're managing one client or ten, QBO keeps you efficient and confident.

Client Communication

Numbers tell a story—but not everyone speaks that language.

Your role is translator: turning complex details into simple clarity that helps clients make smart decisions.

Accuracy builds trust, but empathy keeps it.

When clients feel understood and supported, they stay for years.

Workflow Tools

Stay organized with simple systems and expand as you grow.

Purpose	Tool
Bookkeeping	QuickBooks Online
File Storage	Google Drive / Dropbox
Communication	Gmail + Zoom / Slack / Voxer
Task Tracking	Trello / ClickUp / Google Calendar
Payments	QuickBooks Payments / Stripe
Design	Canva

You don't need expensive software—just structure and consistency.

What You Don't Need

Let's bust a few myths:

- You don't need a CPA license.

- You don't need to be a math genius.

- You don't need a big budget.

- You don't need to know everything before you start.

What you *do* need is courage and consistency.

Every bookkeeper starts at zero, and every skill can be learned.

You're not applying for a job—you're creating one.

Setting Up for Success

Now that you understand the mindset and skills, it's time to put down roots.

Choose Your Business Structure

1. **Sole Proprietor:** fastest start, minimal paperwork.

2. **LLC:** legal protection, simple to register.

3. **S-Corp / C-Corp:** for larger teams—skip for now.

If unsure, start as a sole proprietor and move to an LLC later.

Apply for a free EIN at IRS.gov and use it for banking and contracts.

Open Your Business Bank Account

That first deposit into a dedicated business account changes everything.

Keep business and personal finances separate—it keeps your taxes (and your mindset) clean.

Create Your Workspace

It doesn't need to be fancy—just focused.

A desk, good light, Wi-Fi, and something that reminds you *why* you're doing this.

You're not working from home anymore.

You're working from ownership.

Planning Your First 90 Days

Your first three months set the tone. Don't chase perfection—chase progress.

Month 1 – Learn and Lay Groundwork

- Watch QuickBooks tutorials.

- Create a practice company file.

- Join online bookkeeping communities.

- Share what you're learning—visibility builds courage.

Month 2 – Connect and Clarify

- Identify five local or online businesses.

- Offer a free review of their books to gain practice.

- Ask great questions; listen more than you talk.

- Build proposal and invoice templates.

Month 3 – Deliver and Refine

- Land your first paying client.

- Systemize your workflow.

- Ask for a testimonial.

- Celebrate the win.

Mindset: *Proof beats perfection. One client makes it real.*

Emily's First 90 Days

Emily, a single mom working retail, studied bookkeeping after her kids went to bed.

By week 6 she was cleaning up a bakery's books.

By week 10 the owner handed her a $600 check and said, "You saved me."

She framed the invoice stub.

"It wasn't the money," she said. "It was knowing I could build something that belonged to us."

That's what your first 90 days are about—proof that you can.

Your Rhythm Matters

When you work for yourself, structure replaces supervision.

Set hours you'll keep. Protect them.

Decide when to check email, when to learn, when to rest.

Routine builds momentum. Momentum builds results.

The Foundation of Confidence

Confidence isn't something you wait for—it's something you *build*.

Each small win—forming your LLC, opening your bank account, reconciling your first file—adds a brick to that foundation.

When doubt comes, look back at what you've already built.

You started this from nothing but a decision. That's power.

Mindset Mantras

Keep these close:

- Progress beats perfection.
- Courage first, clarity second.

- I can learn anything I need to know.

- I own my time.

- Done is better than waiting for ready.

Repeat them until they become instinct.

Looking Ahead

You now have the mindset, the tools, and the plan.

Next comes identity—the outward expression of what you've built.

In Chapter 5 – *Branding with Confidence*, we'll craft how the world sees your business: your name, your look, your story, and your online presence.

Because bookkeeping isn't about numbers—it's about **trust**, and trust begins the moment someone encounters your brand.

Take a breath. Look around your workspace.

You're not dreaming anymore. You're building.

And that is the start of life on your terms.

Find free resources, templates, and case studies at
https://stayathomebookkeeper.co/resource.

Chapter 4

Branding with Confidence

The Power of Perception

When you decided to build your own bookkeeping business, you weren't just changing how you make money—you were changing how the world sees you.

And how *you* see yourself.

Branding is more than colors, logos, or fonts.

It's the story people believe about you before you ever say a word.

If Chapter 3 was about *laying the foundation* for your business, this one is about *painting the front door*—making it inviting, trustworthy, and unmistakably yours.

People decide within seconds whether they trust a business. Studies show that more than 90 percent of purchasing decisions are influenced by visuals and emotion rather than facts. That means your brand—the way you look, sound, and show up—matters long before you send a proposal or quote a price.

But branding isn't about pretending to be bigger than you are.

It's about expressing, with confidence, the truth of who you already are and the value you bring.

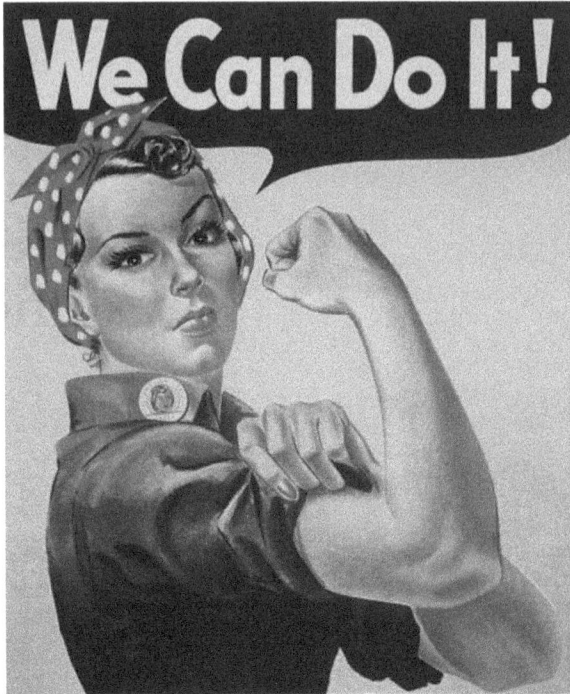

Branding Starts with Belief

Before you design a logo or pick a color, start with mindset.

Because here's the secret: people feel about your business the way you feel about it.

If you present yourself timidly, clients will hesitate.

If you show up proudly, clearly, and consistently, clients relax. They trust you.

You don't need slick marketing or fancy photos—you need authenticity wrapped in clarity.

Confidence is contagious.

That's why this chapter begins with *you*.

The Inner Brand

Every business has two brands:

1. The outer brand – what the world sees (name, visuals, social posts).

2. The inner brand – what you believe about yourself and your work.

Most new business owners skip to the outer brand. They rush to Canva, pick a color, post on Facebook, and wonder why no one responds.

But if the inner brand isn't anchored, the outer one feels hollow.

Your inner brand answers these questions:

- What do I stand for?

- Who am I here to help?

- Why does my work matter?

- What energy do I want people to feel when they interact with me?

When your answers guide everything else—design, words, interactions—you create a brand that's magnetic because it's honest.

Case Study: Amanda's Shift

Amanda started "Ledger Lily Bookkeeping." She loved flowers, so she built her logo around a pink lily.

It was pretty—but generic. Her posts were safe, polite, and forgettable.

During one coaching call, she admitted, "I'm scared to sound like I know what I'm doing. I don't want to come across pushy."

I asked her, "How do you actually feel when you balance someone's books?"

She smiled: "Powerful. Like I'm giving them control of their business again."

We re-framed everything.

New tagline: 'Clarity is Power.'

New tone: direct, encouraging, a bit bold.

Same logo—different energy.

Two weeks later, she landed her biggest client because, as he said, "You sound like you actually care about my numbers."

Your brand begins the moment you claim your power.

Defining Who You Are and What You Stand For

Think of branding as translation.

It translates your personality and purpose into visuals and words the world can understand.

Step 1 – Write Your Brand Story

Your story connects more deeply than any marketing trick.

It's why clients remember you and tell their friends.

Use this simple framework:

1. The Before: Where you were before you started your business.

2. The Turning Point: What made you decide to change.

3. The Mission: Who you help now and why it matters.

4. The Promise: What clients can expect when they work with you.

Example:

"After fifteen years in corporate finance, I wanted my work to mean more than spreadsheets and meetings.

I started Balanced Books Co. to help small-business owners finally understand their numbers and feel confident making decisions.

I believe clarity creates peace—and I bring that peace to every client's business."

That's a story, not a résumé. And people buy stories.

Step 2 – Clarify Your Audience

You can't attract everyone—and you shouldn't try.

Who do you love helping most?

Contractors? Coaches? Boutique owners?

The clearer your audience, the easier it is to speak their language.

When you know who you serve, you know how to design, write, and price with purpose.

Step 3 – Define Your Personality

If your business were a person, how would it behave?

Friendly and relaxed? Professional and precise? Calm and nurturing?

Pick three words that describe your brand's personality.

Mine might be confident, approachable, clear.

Yours might be warm, trustworthy, empowering.

Those words become your compass. Every post, color, or email should feel like *that person.*

Exercise: Your Brand Declaration

Take a blank page and write this sentence, filling in your details:

"I help _____ (audience) to _____ (result or feeling) by _____ (your method or approach)."

Example:

"I help creative entrepreneurs find confidence in their finances by keeping their books clean, clear, and current."

Read it out loud until it feels natural.

That's your brand in one sentence—the seed of every piece of content you'll ever create.

Owning Your Why

Purpose is persuasive.

When people sense that your work means something to you, they trust you faster.

Your "why" doesn't have to be heroic. It just has to be *real.*

Maybe you want to model independence for your kids.

Maybe you want to give families financial peace.

Maybe you simply love the feeling of order after chaos.

Write it down. Frame it near your desk.

Every time you doubt yourself, look at it.

That's your fuel.

Choosing a Name That Fits You

Now that you know who you are and who you help, let's talk about what to call your business.

Names matter—they create first impressions and emotional cues long before someone meets you.

Start with Simplicity

Your business name should be:

- Easy to say

- Easy to spell

- Easy to remember

Avoid puns or overly clever wordplay. If people have to ask how to spell it, they'll forget it.

Your goal is clarity, not cuteness.

Three Types of Effective Names

1. Personal Names

2. Examples: *Sarah J. Bookkeeping, Lisa Rogers Financial Services.*

3. Great for relationship-based businesses. Builds instant trust.

4. Descriptive Names

5. Examples: *Balanced Books Co., Crystal Ledger, Clarity Bookkeeping.*

6. Instantly tell people what you do and the feeling you deliver.

7. Metaphor Names

8. Examples: *North Star Financial, Anchor Ledger, Summit Bookkeeping.*

9. Evoke imagery and emotion—ideal for brands that want to feel modern or creative.

Pick whichever fits your personality best.

Don't overthink—clarity beats clever every time.

Check Availability

Before you fall in love with a name:

1. Search Google and social media to make sure it's not already taken.

2. Visit Namechk.com to check domain and handle availability.

3. Verify your state's business registry if you're forming an LLC.

You want a name you can use everywhere—website, email, Instagram handle—without confusion.

Short Story: "Numbers & Nurture"

When Dee, a former nurse, started her bookkeeping business, she wanted a name that felt as caring as her approach. She called it *Numbers & Nurture.*

Her logo was soft green and cream, colors associated with calm and balance. Her tagline: "Financial care for small business health."

Clients loved it because it felt authentic to her background. They said, "You make bookkeeping feel gentle." That's branding done right—an identity rooted in truth.

Pitfalls to Avoid

- Too Cute: Names like "Bookkeeping Babe" might sound fun now but limit you later.

- Too Corporate: "Global Accounting Enterprises LLC" feels impersonal for a home-based brand.

- Too Vague: "Solutions Unlimited" tells nobody anything.

Choose a name that grows with you and still feels like you ten years from now.

Tagline Magic

A good tagline is like the heartbeat of your brand.

It finishes the sentence your name starts.

Formula:

[Result or Emotion] + [Service or Promise]

Examples:

- *"Clarity for Your Cash Flow."*

- *"Confidence in Every Transaction."*

- *"Numbers Made Simple."*

Keep it under seven words and say it out loud. If it sounds like something you'd naturally say, you're done.

Designing Your Look and Feel

Now that you have a name and a story, it's time to give your brand a face—its *look and feel.*

This is the visual handshake that happens before you ever speak.

Remember: design is communication.

Colors, fonts, and imagery create emotion faster than words can. You don't need to be a designer—you just need intention.

Color Psychology

Colors trigger emotion:

Color	Emotion / Message	When to Use
Blue	Trust, calm, stability	Great for professional, dependable brands
Green	Balance, growth, wellness	Works for bookkeepers who emphasize peace & prosperity
Teal / Aqua	Modern, refreshing, clarity	Perfect for approachable, tech-savvy brands
Gray / White	Clean, minimal, professional	Great accent or background palette
Gold / Mustard	Confidence, success	Use sparingly for highlights or call-to-action

Pick one primary color and one or two supporting tones.

Consistency builds recognition; too many colors build confusion.

Typography & Fonts

Fonts also have personality.

- Sans-serif fonts (like Montserrat, Lato, Open Sans) feel clean, modern, and digital-friendly.

- Serif fonts (like Playfair Display, Merriweather) feel elegant and traditional.

- Script fonts add warmth but use them like perfume—lightly.

Choose no more than two fonts: one for headlines, one for body text.

Keep it legible, especially on mobile.

Imagery & Photography

People connect with faces, not spreadsheets.

Show your workspace, coffee mug, laptop, or smiling photo.

Avoid stock photos of random people in suits shaking hands—it feels cold.

Tip: if you can, schedule a short photo session with a local photographer.

One hour of natural-light photos—typing at your desk, holding a mug, writing notes—can supply you with a year of social-media content.

Creating a Simple Brand Board

Use Canva to assemble:

- Your logo (main and simplified version)
- Color palette (hex codes)
- Fonts

- 3–4 representative photos
- Tagline

This one-page guide keeps your visuals consistent across posts, invoices, and proposals.

Consistency whispers *professional* even when you're a team of one.

Story: Rachel's Rebrand

Rachel launched "Reliable Books LLC." Her work was excellent, but her visuals were gray and outdated. "Reliable" sounded solid—but not exciting.

She decided to refresh: new name "Clarity Ledger", deep-teal palette, and a clean word-mark logo.

Within two months her inquiries doubled. Clients said, "You look like you know exactly who you are."

Same Rachel. Same skills. A brand that finally matched her energy.

That's the power of alignment.

Crafting Your Online Presence

Your brand lives where people meet you—online.

But you don't need to build a complex website before you build trust. Start with what's fast and free: social media.

Facebook & Instagram

These are your story-telling platforms.

Post about:

- Client wins (with permission).
- Lessons learned.
- Behind-the-scenes snapshots of your workday.
- Encouragement for small-business owners.

Visual rule: use your brand colors in every post—either background, text, or photo tone.

It trains people's brains to recognize you instantly.

LinkedIn

LinkedIn is your digital business card.

Update:

- Headline → "Helping small-business owners gain financial clarity through modern bookkeeping."

- About section → your brand story + a simple call to action ("Message me to schedule a clarity call.")

- Banner image → your tagline in brand colors.

Post twice a week: quick tips, client stories, or motivational thoughts about entrepreneurship.

Email

Create a professional email: *yourname@yourbusiness.com*.

Even if your business is tiny, a branded email elevates credibility.

Gmail's domain tools make this simple.

Website (Phase 2)

Once you've landed 2–3 clients, build a one-page site:

- Logo & tagline at top

- "About You" section (your story)

- "Services" (clear list—monthly bookkeeping, cleanup, payroll)

- Testimonials

- Contact form

Keep it light, clear, mobile-friendly.

A confused visitor never becomes a client.

Posting with Purpose

Ask before every post: *Does this help, teach, or inspire?*

If not, skip it.

Content ideas:

- "3 ways to know if your books are healthy."

- "What I wish every small-business owner knew about cash flow."

- "Why reconciling monthly saves stress at tax time."

Your content is not about proving expertise; it's about proving you *care*.

Networking and Referrals as Part of Your Brand

Your brand isn't confined to visuals. It's how you show up in conversations.

Every interaction—DMs, Zoom calls, community groups—is brand communication.

The Know-Like-Trust Factor

People do business with people they:

1. Know – they've seen your name before.

2. Like – your tone feels genuine.

3. Trust – you follow through.

Branding accelerates all three.

When you consistently show up with kindness, clarity, and value, referrals multiply naturally.

Simple Introduction Script

"Hi [name], I'm [Your Name]. I help small-business owners stay organized and confident by keeping their books clean and clear. I love supporting [niche] businesses like yours—would you be open to connecting?"

That's it. Friendly, not salesy.

Local Presence

Even if you work virtually, claim your hometown pride.

Join your Chamber of Commerce or local business Facebook group.

Sponsor a coffee meetup or offer a free workshop called "Bookkeeping Basics for Non-Numbers People."

People remember faces more than flyers.

Your Brand in Conversation

Imagine meeting someone new.

They ask, "What do you do?"

Most new entrepreneurs shrink in that moment.

They mumble, "Oh, I just do some bookkeeping from home."

Stop saying *just*.

Try this instead:

"I own a virtual bookkeeping business. I help small-business owners feel confident about their finances."

See the difference? Same truth. Different energy.

Confidence sells itself.

The Confidence Loop

When you *look* the part, you *feel* the part—and when you feel it, you act it.

Every time you post consistently, show up professionally, or hand out a polished business card, you reinforce the identity of "successful business owner."

That's why branding is more than marketing—it's mindset practice in disguise.

Story: Lena's Leap

Lena hesitated to announce her new business online. "What if people think I'm bragging?"

We reframed it: "What if people need the help you can give?"

She posted her story—why she started, what she believed about small-business finance—and added her new logo.

Within two days, five messages arrived. One was from her former coworker, now her first paying client.

When you declare who you are, the world responds.

Daily Brand Habits

1. Consistency – show up the same way across all channels.

2. Clarity – avoid jargon; speak human.

3. Connection – reply to every comment or message.

4. Confidence – don't apologize for selling; you're solving problems.

5. Care – put genuine gratitude into every interaction.

Your habits become your reputation.

Refreshing Your Brand Over Time

Brands evolve as we do.

Every 12–18 months, audit yours:

- Does my message still reflect my purpose?

- Do my visuals still match my audience?

- Do I still feel proud when I see my logo?

If the answer to any of those is *no,* update.

Change isn't inconsistency—it's growth.

Mini Checklist: Brand Essentials

- ☑ Clear, memorable name
- ☑ Professional email address
- ☑ Simple logo & color palette
- ☑ One-sentence brand declaration
- ☑ Social-media presence (LinkedIn + one more)
- ☑ Consistent tone & message
- ☑ Confidence

If you have these, you're already miles ahead of most startups.

Preparing for Chapter 5 – Bringing Tech and AI Into Your Brand

You now have a voice, a look, and a presence that reflect who you are.

Next, we'll add tools that help you maintain that presence without burning out.

In Chapter 5 – Leveraging AI for Growth and Simplicity, you'll discover how to:

- Use AI to write posts, emails, and proposals in *your* voice.

- Automate repetitive marketing tasks so your brand stays visible.

- Keep consistency and creativity without constant stress.

Because branding isn't a one-time project—it's an ongoing conversation between you and the world.

And the smarter your systems, the easier that conversation becomes.

Take a moment now. Look at your name, your colors, your story.

That's you—visible, confident, professional.

You've built a brand that tells the truth about your best self.

And that's where real business begins.

Additional resources, case studies, forms, and more are waiting for you at https://stayathomebookkeeper.co/resource. Visit the site now and enjoy a huge collection of resources that are absolutely free!

Chapter 5

Leveraging AI for Growth and Simplicity

The Rise of Smart Tools

There's a quiet revolution happening in business—and you're standing at the perfect doorway to join it.

Artificial Intelligence used to sound like science fiction. Today it's as common as a search bar. We talk to it, write with it, design through it, and schedule around it.

For most small-business owners, AI feels mysterious: a buzzword, an app they "should look into someday." But for you—as a new bookkeeping entrepreneur—it's the simplest, fastest way to multiply your time, polish your brand, and expand what's possible without working more hours.

AI isn't replacing people who care. It's replacing busywork.

Think of it like this: in the same way calculators freed accountants from long division, modern AI frees bookkeepers from tedious marketing, repetitive messages, and endless formatting. It turns the tasks that drain you into the ones that *train* your business to run smoothly.

Why Now Is the Moment

Ten years ago, most automation required expensive software.

Now, the tools are free or nearly free—and built for small business.

ChatGPT can write your client emails.

Canva's Magic Write can draft captions that match your tone.

QuickBooks Online now flags anomalies automatically.

Zapier can connect your calendar, CRM, and invoicing so everything syncs.

When you learn how to use these helpers, your one-person bookkeeping shop suddenly runs with the efficiency of a small team.

Technology is finally small-business friendly. And that means leverage.

Reframing AI as Your Partner, Not Your Replacement

The first mindset hurdle most bookkeepers face is fear:

"If AI can do so much, will it make me obsolete?"

Absolutely not.

AI can count data, but it can't care.

It can summarize numbers, but it can't empathize with a stressed business owner staring at those numbers.

The secret to thriving in an AI world is realizing that *people still buy people*. They hire you because you listen, explain, and simplify. AI just amplifies your impact.

Think of AI as Your Apprentice

Imagine hiring a tireless assistant who:

- Works 24/7.

- Never complains.

- Produces drafts and ideas instantly.

- Costs less than a latte per day.

That's what AI is. It's your creative apprentice—brilliant but literal.

You provide the heart and direction; it provides speed and structure.

You wouldn't hand a new assistant your entire client list on day one; you'd train them. Do the same with AI. Give it clear instructions, review its work, and refine. Over time, it learns your rhythm.

The Human Edge

Empathy, integrity, tone, trust—these can't be automated.

AI can generate words; it can't generate *warmth*.

That's why your role as a modern bookkeeper actually becomes more valuable: you combine precision with personality.

Technology should never replace the human handshake—it should extend it.

Story: Melissa and the Email Block

Melissa ran her home-based bookkeeping business smoothly—except for one thing. She dreaded writing follow-up emails. Weeks of invoices sat unsent because she overthought every word.

One day she opened ChatGPT and typed:

"Write a polite, professional email reminding a small-business client that their invoice is overdue by ten days. Keep the tone friendly but firm."

Seconds later, she had a perfect draft. She adjusted a few details and sent it. The client paid that afternoon.

"That one email saved me three hours of stress," she says. "Now I use AI for almost everything I used to procrastinate."

Melissa didn't lose authenticity; she gained momentum.

Where AI Saves You Time

Let's break down exactly where AI fits into a bookkeeper's world.

Think of four main categories: Marketing, Communication, Client Experience, and Workflow.

1. Marketing Made Manageable

Bookkeepers often say, "I'm great with numbers, not words."

AI bridges that gap.

Content Creation Made Simple

- Social Posts:

- Prompt:

  "Write a short, upbeat LinkedIn post for a bookkeeping business about why reconciling monthly saves time at tax season. Use a friendly tone."

Edit the output until it sounds like you. Add your photo or brand colors. Done.

- Blog or Newsletter Ideas:

- Ask:

  "Give me ten article titles about financial organization for small-business owners."

  Choose one. Let AI draft the outline. Then add your real-world perspective.

- Canva Magic Write:

- Inside Canva, open a design → click *Magic Write* → describe what you need ("five caption ideas about cash-flow confidence").

- In seconds, you have post captions that match your visuals.

Consistency builds trust. AI makes consistency realistic.

2. Client Communication Without the Overwhelm

AI helps you write faster while keeping your personal tone.

Common uses:

- Welcome emails for new clients.

- Meeting summaries.

- Monthly check-in messages.

- Polite reminders for documents or payments.

Prompt Template:

"Write a [length] message to [audience] about [topic]. Tone: [friendly / confident / professional]. Include a call to action asking them to [next step]."

You'll be amazed how well this works as a starting point. You remain the editor—the human who adds empathy and nuance.

Story: David's Monthly Updates

David, a virtual bookkeeper with ten clients, used to spend an entire Friday writing monthly summaries.

He asked ChatGPT:

"Create a 150-word summary email for a client whose revenue increased 15 percent this month. Congratulate them, mention improved expense tracking, and encourage them to keep up the momentum."

He pasted real numbers into the draft, personalized two sentences, and sent it.

"Now I finish all my updates before lunch," he laughs. "Clients think I hired a writer."

3. Client Experience and Education

AI helps you educate clients—one of the most valuable parts of your service.

Try prompts like:

"Explain in simple terms why reconciling accounts monthly prevents tax-time stress. Use everyday language."

"Write a friendly FAQ for new bookkeeping clients answering common questions about QuickBooks access and document sharing."

You can paste the results into onboarding guides, proposals, or your website. It makes you look polished and proactive.

When clients feel informed, they trust you more—and that's priceless.

4. Workflow and Organization

Automation connects your systems so work happens while you sleep.

Zapier is your invisible assistant.

Example Zaps:

- When a new client signs your online contract → create a folder in Google Drive.

- When a client pays an invoice → mark project "complete" in Trello.

- When you receive a lead form → send a thank-you email automatically.

QuickBooks Online AI already performs smart tasks:

- Auto-categorizing transactions based on past behavior.

- Flagging duplicate entries.

- Predicting cash-flow trends.

You remain the expert; the software simply reduces manual clicks.

Time Math:

If AI saves you just one hour per client per month and you have six clients, that's 72 hours per year—almost two full work-weeks.

That's time you can reinvest in marketing, learning, or family.

The Confidence Behind the Tech

Using AI doesn't mean you're cheating. It means you're optimizing.

You're not paid for how long a task takes—you're paid for the value it creates.

Clients care that their books are accurate, their questions answered, and their experience smooth. They don't care whether you used a notepad or a neural network to get there.

The sooner you embrace this truth, the faster your business grows.

Real-World Prompt Examples for Bookkeepers

Situation	Sample Prompt to Start
Welcome email	"Write a friendly welcome message for a new bookkeeping client outlining next steps and emphasizing organization and transparency."
Testimonial request	"Draft a short email asking a satisfied client for a testimonial. Tone: warm, appreciative, easy to answer."
Blog intro	"Write an engaging opening paragraph for a blog post titled 'Why Cash Flow Matters More Than Profit.' Keep it under 100 words."
Proposal polish	"Improve this paragraph to sound confident and client-focused: [paste text]."
Social caption	"Give me three Instagram captions (under 100 words) about the peace of mind bookkeeping provides to small-business owners."

You'll rarely use an output word-for-word—but 70 percent of the work is done instantly.

AI in Your Brand Voice

When you trained your brand in the last chapter, you defined personality words: friendly, trustworthy, empowering.

Feed those into every AI prompt:

"Write in a friendly, empowering tone that sounds conversational, like a mentor helping a peer."

Over time, the AI learns your rhythm. Save your favorite prompts in a "brand voice" document to reuse later.

The goal is not to sound robotic—it's to sound like the *best, most polished version of you.*

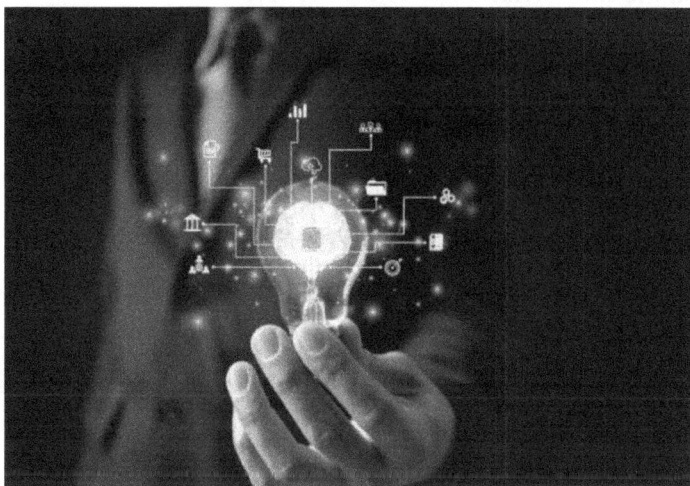

The Essential Tools and Prompts

You don't need to master every new platform.

Start with a short, powerful toolkit that covers writing, design, bookkeeping automation, and connection.

1. ChatGPT – Your Everyday Assistant

Think of ChatGPT as your brainstorming partner.

You can use it to:

- Draft client emails or proposals.

- Create marketing ideas.

- Build checklists or onboarding templates.

- Simplify explanations for clients.

Prompt Starter Kit

"Act as a friendly bookkeeping expert. Write a 150-word explanation of why accurate categorization saves tax money."

"Summarize this paragraph in plain English: [paste text]."

"Give me five social-media post ideas about financial confidence for small-business owners."

Always edit the results. You are the voice; AI is the keyboard that types faster than you can.

2. Canva Magic Write & Brand Kit

Inside Canva, open any design, click Magic Write, and describe what you need:

"Create three caption ideas for Instagram about how clean books create peace of mind."

Then drop the text into a branded template.

The Brand Kit feature stores your logo, fonts, and colors so every post feels consistent.

Consistency = professionalism = trust.

3. QuickBooks Online AI

QuickBooks has quietly become an AI platform.

It learns from your habits—categorizing transactions automatically, flagging anomalies, and predicting cash-flow trends.

The result: fewer clicks, faster close-outs.

Use that time to deepen client relationships or work on your business instead of in it.

4. Zapier (or Make /Integromat)

These tools connect your apps like invisible wires.

Examples:

- When a new client signs your Dubsado contract → create a Google Drive folder automatically.

- When someone fills out your lead form → send a pre-written welcome email.

- When you post a blog → share it on LinkedIn automatically.

One hour of setup can save dozens every month.

5. Grammarly and Notion AI

Grammarly polishes every email and proposal so you sound crisp but kind.

Notion AI helps organize ideas, summarize meeting notes, and draft SOPs for your growing team.

Use them quietly behind the scenes; your clients only notice how clear and consistent you've become.

Building Authentic Automation

Automation doesn't mean cold or mechanical.

It means freeing your attention for the human parts of business that matter most.

Start Small

Automate repetitive tasks first:

- Scheduling reminders.

- Follow-up emails.

- Invoice notifications.

Every automation you add should answer the question: *Does this improve the client experience or my peace of mind?*

If it doesn't serve one of those, skip it.

Keep the Human Touch

Automate delivery, not emotion.

You can schedule a "Happy Birthday" message, but you still write it yourself.

You can automate invoice follow-ups, but add a line that sounds like you: *"Hope your week's going well, here's this month's summary."*

Automation should sound like a person who cares—because it's you behind it.

Boundaries Through Systems

AI also protects your time.

You can set up autoresponders that politely manage expectations:

"Thanks for reaching out! I check email Monday–Thursday and will reply within 24 hours."

That single sentence removes guilt from your evenings.

Automation creates boundaries—and boundaries protect burnout.

Story: Laura's Turnaround

Laura juggled six clients and felt like she was drowning in admin work.

She spent nights typing the same reminders and scheduling the same tasks.

After setting up three simple automations—Zapier for onboarding, ChatGPT templates for emails, and QuickBooks auto-rules—she cut her admin time in half.

"I didn't hire help," she says. "I built it."

Her energy returned, and so did her weekends.

That's authentic automation: systems that serve your humanity, not replace it.

The Freedom Multiplier

The true promise of AI isn't more technology—it's *more life*.

When you delegate the mechanical parts of your work, you reclaim the creative ones.

Picture what you could do with ten extra hours a week:

- Spend an afternoon mentoring your child.

- Take Fridays off.

- Plan growth instead of chasing deadlines.

Freedom doesn't appear all at once; it builds in minutes saved.

AI gives you those minutes back.

Measure the Win

Start tracking tasks you've automated. Each month, list:

- Time saved.

- Stress reduced.

- Revenue gained.

When you see those numbers, you'll never feel guilty for using technology again.

Your Ethical Compass

You'll sometimes hear skeptics say, "AI is lazy."

It isn't. Misuse is lazy; leverage is wise.

Use AI to:

- ☑ Save time, not hide dishonesty.
- ☑ Enhance creativity, not erase your voice.
- ☑ Support clarity, not mislead.

Always double-check facts, protect client data, and disclose tools when appropriate.

Your integrity is your most valuable algorithm.

Story: Sam's Next Level

Sam built his bookkeeping firm to six clients but couldn't break the ceiling.

He spent hours per week writing proposals and social posts.

After integrating ChatGPT for drafts and Zapier for lead management, he gained five hours weekly.

He used that time to attend local meetups—landing three new clients.

"AI didn't replace me," he says. "It promoted me."

That's the freedom multiplier at work: turning efficiency into expansion.

Daily AI Routine (Sample)

Time	Task	Tool
8:00 am	Check QuickBooks dashboard	QBO AI alerts
9:00 am	Generate daily to-do list	ChatGPT prompt: "Summarize today's priorities based on ..."
11:00 am	Design one social post	Canva Magic Write + Brand Kit
2:00 pm	Automate invoice follow-ups	Zapier workflow
4:00 pm	Draft newsletter paragraph	ChatGPT + Grammarly review

That's one hour of setup for a day that flows effortlessly.

Your AI Learning Curve

Treat every new tool like a short course: explore for 15 minutes a day.

Experiment. Fail safely. Adjust.

Confidence comes from use, not theory.

Within a month, you'll find yourself saying, "Why didn't I do this sooner?"

Transition to Chapter 6 – Building Client Relationships That Last

You now understand how technology becomes your teammate.

But tech is only half of long-term success.

The next chapter brings us back to the human side—the art of connection, trust, and loyalty that turns clients into advocates.

In Chapter 6 – Building Client Relationships That Last, you'll learn:

- How to communicate with warmth and authority.

- How to retain clients through clarity and care.

- How to use automation to support, not substitute, real relationships.

Because the future of bookkeeping isn't just smart—it's deeply human.

AI gives you time; relationships give you purpose.

Additional resources, case studies, forms, and more are waiting for you at https://stayathomebookkeeper.co/resource. Visit the site now and enjoy a huge collection of resources that are absolutely free!

Chapter 6

Building Client
Relationships That Last

Why Relationships Are the Real ROI

Technology changes fast. People don't.

Every app, automation, or clever system you use means nothing if the people behind the numbers don't feel cared for.

The most successful bookkeepers I know aren't the ones with the most certifications or the fanciest software. They're the ones whose clients light up when their name pops into an inbox. They've built relationships rooted in trust, consistency, and calm.

Your clients aren't just paying for reconciled accounts—they're paying for peace of mind.

They want to sleep at night knowing someone competent and kind is watching over their finances. That's the hidden heartbeat of this business.

When you grasp that, everything changes. You stop chasing "more clients" and start cultivating *better* ones.

The result?

- Fewer one-off projects, more long-term retainers.

- Less marketing stress, more referrals.

- Predictable income and the priceless satisfaction of being indispensable.

Retention beats acquisition every time. It costs roughly five times more to win a new client than to keep an existing one—and loyal clients become your best marketing team.

So, while technology keeps the gears turning, relationships keep the business alive.

The Trust Equation

Trust isn't built through grand gestures. It's built through quiet reliability repeated over time.

I like to define it like this:

Consistency + Communication + Care = Confidence.

Let's unpack that.

Consistency

Your clients notice the little things: replies within a day, reports that arrive when promised, tone that stays professional even on hard days.

Consistency says, *"You can count on me."*

Deliver on what you promise, even if what you promise is simple:

"I'll send this Friday." Then send it Friday.

Consistency is the slow-burn proof of credibility. It builds equity that no marketing campaign can buy.

Communication

Clear communication prevents 90 percent of client problems.

Be proactive:

- Send monthly updates, even if nothing major happened.

- Explain what you're doing in plain English.

- Ask before assuming.

A quick "Hey, I saw a new vendor on your statement—want me to code that under supplies?" takes seconds and reinforces transparency.

When people feel informed, they relax. And relaxed clients stay.

Care

Care is the secret ingredient that turns service into loyalty.

You can't fake genuine interest in your client's success.

Ask about their goals. Celebrate their wins. When their business anniversary comes up, send a simple "Congrats on another year!" email.

That tiny act says you see them as humans, not invoices.

Combine those three—Consistency, Communication, and Care—and you create *Confidence*.

That confidence is what clients actually buy.

The Client Journey

Think of every client relationship as a story with chapters.

When you understand what clients need emotionally at each stage, you meet them where they are—and they stay for the sequel.

1. Inquiry – First Impression

This is where curiosity meets caution. They're thinking, *"Can I trust this person with my books?"*

Your job isn't to impress; it's to reassure.

Respond quickly. Answer clearly. Show calm authority.

You might say:

"Thanks for reaching out! Let's schedule a short call to see what systems you're using and what's working well. I'll walk you through my process so you know exactly what to expect."

No pressure, no jargon—just partnership. They should leave the conversation thinking, *"That was easy."*

Mini-Story – Tanya's First Call

Tanya used to rush discovery calls, listing services like a résumé. After one prospect ghosted, she changed her approach: she started every call with, "Tell me about your business."

The next client talked for fifteen minutes straight—and signed on the spot. People don't hire résumés; they hire listeners.

2. Onboarding – The Trust Launch

Once they say yes, your next move sets the tone for everything. Clients should feel guided, not overwhelmed.

Create a short checklist or welcome packet that answers:

- What happens next

- When they'll hear from you

- How to send documents securely

- When to expect their first report

Automation helps here, but always add a human note.

"I'm excited to partner with you. You'll receive a quick setup form tomorrow, and I'll check in mid-week to be sure everything's clear."

That message, warm and predictable, lowers anxiety instantly.

Tip: Record a 90-second welcome video in Canva or Loom. Smile. Say hi. Walk them through what's next. Face-to-face connection builds trust faster than paragraphs.

3. Service – Delivering Peace

Once the workflow starts, your goal is stability.

This is where the Trust Equation plays out daily.

Schedule routine updates:

- Monthly email summary ("Here's what we accomplished this month").

- Quarterly review ("You're trending up 12 %—great job!").

- Occasional check-in call.

Predictability turns transactions into relationships.

Remember: what feels repetitive to you feels reliable to them.

4. Renewal – Reassure and Recommit

Before contracts expire or projects end, start the renewal conversation early.

"We're coming up on the end of our six-month agreement. I'd love to review what's working and map out next steps for the next quarter."

This simple invitation communicates foresight and partnership. Most clients renew automatically when they sense you're thinking ahead.

5. Advocacy – From Clients to Champions

Happy clients talk.

Encourage them—gently—to share their experience.

Send a short note:

"I've loved working with you this quarter. If you know another business that could use a little more financial clarity, would you mind introducing us?"

Make it easy for them to recommend you.

A link, a one-sentence blurb, a quick thank-you gift card—all small touches that spark big loyalty.

Story – Harper's Circle

Harper, a virtual bookkeeper in Oregon, built her entire client base through referrals. She never ran ads.

Her secret? Every December she mailed handwritten cards thanking clients for their partnership and highlighting one thing she admired about their business. No sales pitch, just sincerity.

By February, her calendar filled through word-of-mouth.

People remember gratitude.

Communication That Connects

Bookkeeping may deal in numbers, but relationships thrive on words.

How you communicate shapes how clients feel about working with you.

The Art of Being Clear and Kind

Every message you send—email, text, report—should answer three questions for your client:

1. *What happened?*

2. *What does it mean?*

3. *What should I do next?*

The more you remove uncertainty, the more you earn trust.

Keep messages short and structured.

Start with gratitude ("Thanks for sending that statement!"), explain the issue clearly, and end with direction ("Please confirm by Thursday").

Clients don't remember every detail—they remember how you made things feel simple.

Transparency Builds Safety

Never leave clients guessing.

If a project is delayed, tell them early. If you spot a potential problem, flag it immediately. Transparency might feel scary in the moment, but it always deepens respect.

"I noticed a discrepancy in last month's payroll records. I'm reviewing it now and will send you a clear report by tomorrow."

That's professional calm. It shows accountability, not anxiety.

Listening More Than You Talk

Numbers are logical, but people are emotional.

When clients vent, they're rarely just talking about finances—they're talking about fear.

Listen. Pause. Reflect back what you heard:

"It sounds like the cash flow dip last month really worried you. Let's look at the patterns together."

You don't have to fix every problem immediately. Sometimes clients just need reassurance that someone is paying attention.

Using AI & Automation to Support Relationships

Technology can quietly strengthen your human touch when used wisely.

1. Staying Present Without Being Glued to the Screen

Automate routine updates so clients never feel forgotten.

Set reminders or use Zapier to:

- Send monthly check-ins ("Your latest report is ready—want to schedule a quick review?").
- Trigger welcome emails for new clients.
- Schedule birthday or business anniversary notes.

Automation isn't cold—it's considerate.

It ensures no client slips through the cracks.

2. Drafting with AI, Personalizing with Heart

Let ChatGPT or Grammarly handle the first draft of your messages, then layer your warmth on top.

Example prompt:

"Write a friendly, encouraging email reminding a small-business client to upload their receipts for reconciliation. Keep tone casual but professional."

Then add a line only *you* could write:

"Hope your new product launch is going well—can't wait to see the numbers next month!"

AI provides structure; you provide soul.

3. Keeping a Record of Care

Use Notion or Google Sheets to track human touches: birthdays, milestones, preferences.

Add a column labeled "Last Personal Message."

Update it monthly.

That way, your follow-ups are intentional, not accidental.

Turning Clients into Advocates

When a client moves from satisfied to *delighted*, they become an ambassador for your brand.

1. Celebrate Their Wins

Every quarter, send a short note highlighting progress:

"You increased revenue 12% this quarter while cutting expenses by 5%. That's fantastic! Thanks for letting me be part of your journey."

You're not just their bookkeeper—you're their partner in growth.

2. Ask for Testimonials Naturally

Timing is everything. The best moment to ask is right after a positive outcome.

Say:

"I'm so glad the cleanup project went smoothly. If you're comfortable, could you share a few sentences about what it was like working together? It helps other small-business owners feel confident getting help, too."

Make it easy. Include a link or simple form.

3. Reward Referrals

A thank-you note or small gift card shows appreciation.

You're not buying loyalty—you're acknowledging partnership.

4. Build Community

Create a simple quarterly email newsletter that celebrates your clients collectively.

Feature their businesses ("Client Spotlight"), share quick tips, or include motivational quotes about entrepreneurship.

It turns a service list into a network.

Stories of Connection

Harper's "Friday Thank-You" Habit

Harper, a bookkeeper from Colorado, started sending one thank-you message every Friday.

Sometimes it was an email, sometimes a text: *"Hey, loved working on your account this week—hope your weekend's great."*

Within six months, two clients referred her to new businesses simply because "You're the only person who checks in just to say thanks."

Gratitude travels further than advertising.

Miguel and the Late-Night Call

Miguel's client called panicked one night: "The IRS sent a letter—I think we're in trouble."

Miguel calmly reviewed the issue, explained it was a minor form update, and emailed a solution the same evening.

The next day, the client said, "You saved me from a sleepless night."

A ten-minute response built lifetime loyalty.

The Balance of Boundaries and Service

Strong relationships need both warmth and structure.

Without boundaries, generosity turns into exhaustion.

1. Set Clear Availability

Define your working hours—and stick to them.

Include them in your onboarding packet and email signature.

Clients respect clarity:

"I'm available Monday through Thursday, 9–4. If you message outside those hours, I'll respond the next business day."

That single sentence eliminates 80% of after-hours stress.

2. Say "No" with Grace

Every business reaches a point where not every client is a fit.

Saying no isn't rejection—it's protection.

You can decline with kindness:

"I don't think my services are the best fit for what you need, but I can recommend a trusted colleague."

Boundaries attract the right clients.

When you respect your limits, others do too.

3. The Power of Pause

Never answer a difficult message in the heat of emotion.

Pause, breathe, step away.

Clarity is your superpower.

A calm, thoughtful response beats a fast one every time.

The Relationship Flywheel

Once you create systems of consistency, communication, and care, your business begins to feed itself.

Here's how it flows:

1. You show up consistently.

2. Clients trust you more.

3. They refer others.

4. Your calendar fills.

5. You can be selective, serving people you truly enjoy.

This is the sweet spot of a mature bookkeeping business—one built not on chasing clients, but on nurturing them.

Transition to Chapter 7 – Scaling Beyond Yourself

You've learned how to create a business rooted in trust, clarity, and authentic connection.

Next, we'll look at how to expand that success without sacrificing your balance.

In Chapter 7 – Scaling Beyond Yourself, you'll discover:

- How to decide when and how to hire help.

- Systems that grow with you.

- The mindset shift from bookkeeper to business owner to CEO.

Because freedom isn't just working for yourself—it's learning how to grow *beyond* yourself.

Additional resources, case studies, forms, and more are waiting for you at https://stayathomebookkeeper.co/resource. Visit the site now and enjoy a huge collection of resources that are absolutely free!

Chapter 7

Scaling Beyond Yourself

The Moment You Outgrow "Solo"

Every business reaches a point where hard work stops being the answer.

At first, growth feels like excitement—new clients, steady revenue, glowing testimonials.

Then, one morning, you realize you're juggling twelve inboxes, living in QuickBooks, and answering emails at midnight. You're grateful and exhausted at the same time.

That's the moment you've outgrown "solo."

It's a strange season: you're successful enough to be busy but not yet free enough to breathe. The systems that once worked now strain under the weight of success.

This isn't failure; it's evolution.

The purpose of this chapter is to help you step confidently into your next identity—not just as a bookkeeper, but as a business owner with leverage, leadership, and longevity.

The Emotional Shift

Scaling isn't just operational; it's emotional.

Most bookkeepers start their businesses for freedom and quickly realize that control can become another cage. The instinct is to hold everything close:

"It's faster if I do it myself."

"I can't afford help yet."

"No one will care like I do."

Those are understandable thoughts—and they're all short-term traps.

The truth is, freedom expands only when you learn to share responsibility. You don't lose control; you multiply it. Delegation done right gives you more creative control, not less.

The people who stay "solo forever" eventually hit a ceiling—not of income, but of energy. The ones who learn to let go step into entirely new possibilities.

Redefining Growth

Growth doesn't have to mean more clients, more chaos, or more stress.

It can mean *better* clients, smoother operations, and smarter pricing.

Scaling is about sustainability—building a business that works even when you're not glued to your desk.

Start asking new questions:

- "How can this happen without me?"

- "What if I built systems that could serve 20 clients as easily as two?"

- "Where is my time best spent?"

These are the questions CEOs ask. And the sooner you start thinking that way, the easier scaling becomes.

Thinking Like a CEO

The difference between a bookkeeper and a CEO isn't talent—it's focus.

Bookkeepers focus on *doing the work.*

CEOs focus on *building the system* that gets the work done.

The Leverage Mindset

Leverage means achieving more with less effort.

There are only three levers in any business:

1. People – delegating tasks that drain you.

2. Process – standardizing repeatable actions.

3. Technology – automating steps that don't need a human touch.

Every hour you spend documenting, delegating, or automating creates hours you'll never have to work again.

Ask yourself weekly: *Is this something only I can do?*

If not, systematize or delegate it.

Delegating Outcomes, Not Tasks

When you eventually bring help onboard—whether a virtual assistant, junior bookkeeper, or contractor—don't just hand them random assignments.

Give them ownership of outcomes.

Example:

Instead of saying,

"Enter these 200 transactions."

Say,

"Make sure all bank transactions for Client A are reconciled by Friday, categorized accurately, and ready for my review."

That subtle shift turns an assistant into a partner. You're hiring thinkers, not button-pushers.

Story – Talia's Turning Point

Talia ran a thriving solo practice for four years. She managed twelve clients, handled every report, and prided herself on never missing a deadline.

Then burnout hit.

One night she looked at her computer clock—2 a.m.—and thought, *"I built another job, not a business."*

She started documenting everything she did for one client – screen recordings, checklists, email templates.

Three weeks later she hired a part-time VA to handle document requests and client emails. Within two months, her workload dropped 30 percent and revenue rose because she finally had time to onboard two new clients.

"That was the moment I became a CEO," she says.

The Power of Perspective

CEOs zoom out. They spend as much time thinking *about* the business as they do working *in* it.

Block an hour each week for strategy: review your client list, revenue, and energy levels.

Ask:

- Which clients energize me?
- Which processes drain me?
- What bottleneck keeps recurring?

That hour of reflection prevents weeks of frustration.

Remember: clarity is a form of leverage.

Systems Before Staff

Most people think scaling starts with hiring. It doesn't.

It starts with systems.

Why Systems First

Hiring without systems is like adding passengers to a boat before patching the leaks.

Systems make work repeatable, measurable, and teachable.

They let new people succeed without constant supervision.

They also give you visibility—so you can manage by results, not guesses.

Document Everything Once

For the next 30 days, treat yourself as your own employee.

As you work, record or write down every recurring task:

Task	Frequency	Tool	Notes
Reconcile accounts	Weekly	QuickBooks	Checklist saved in Google Drive
Send client updates	Monthly	Gmail + Canva template	Use "Monthly Update" email draft
Request bank statements	Monthly	Dubsado form	Triggered via automation

After a month, you'll see your entire workflow mapped out. That's your foundation for delegation.

Use Loom or Zoom Recordings

Record yourself completing tasks while narrating the steps.

Store those short videos in a "Training Library."

When you eventually bring on help, you'll already have built your own onboarding program.

Create Simple SOPs (Standard Operating Procedures)

SOPs sound corporate but they're simply *recipes* for success.

Each one answers three questions:

1. What is the goal?

2. What steps get us there?

3. How do we know it's done right?

Example SOP Outline:

Task: Monthly Client Reconciliation

Goal: Ensure all transactions are categorized and reconciled by the 5th of each month.

Steps:

1. Login to QuickBooks.

2. Import bank feeds.

3. Review transactions and categorize.

4. Check uncleared items.

5. Send summary email to client for confirmation.

6. Quality Check: Balance sheet and bank statement match; email sent and saved in folder.

Keep SOPs short – one page each.

They should empower, not overwhelm.

Automate Before You Hire

AI and automation can often replace a part-time assistant in the early stages.

Examples:

- Use Zapier to create folders and send welcome emails automatically.

- Schedule monthly reminders in ClickUp.

- Let QuickBooks auto-categorize routine transactions.

Automation creates the breathing room you'll need to train real people later.

Story – Erin's System Shift

Erin was ready to hire but realized her processes existed only in her head.

She spent two weeks documenting every step of her client onboarding process and built simple checklists in Trello.

By the time she hired her assistant, training took two days instead of two months.

"I used to think systems were boring," she laughs. "Now I see they're freedom disguised as checklists."

The System Rule of Three

Whenever you repeat a task three times, systematize it.

That simple rule forces you to capture processes before they spiral.

Write a checklist, create a template, record a walkthrough.

Your future self will thank you when you're training someone new.

Protect Your Client Experience

As you build systems, always test them through the client's eyes.

Ask: *Does this feel organized and personal?*

Efficiency means nothing if clients feel like numbers.

Every automation should end with a human touch—an email signature with warm language, a check-in call, a simple "thanks for sending that so quickly!"

System + Sincerity = Scalability with soul.

Hiring Help the Smart Way

Once your systems run smoothly, you're ready for people to run them.

Hiring doesn't mean building a big company overnight—it means buying back time intentionally.

Start with Support, Not Supervision

The first hire most bookkeepers need isn't another bookkeeper—it's a helper who removes friction.

Think:

- A virtual assistant to manage scheduling and email.
- A contractor for social media or newsletter tasks.
- A part-time bookkeeper to handle reconciliations under your review.

Start small.

Choose one recurring task that drains energy and hand it off.

You'll feel the relief immediately.

How to Find Good People

1. Referrals First. Ask peers, business groups, or your Academy network.
2. Trial Projects. Give candidates one paid task before long-term commitment.

3. Values Fit. Skill can be taught; integrity can't.

Look for these signs: reliability, curiosity, kindness, and clear communication.

Those qualities beat technical perfection every time.

Onboarding New Team Members

Bring them into your world gently.

- Share your mission and vision ("We give clients peace, not panic.").

- Walk them through your SOPs.

- Record a short welcome video outlining expectations and encouragement.

Check in during the first two weeks, then shift from managing to mentoring.

Delegation Checklist

☑ The task is clearly defined.

☑ There's a written process or video tutorial.

☑ You've set deadlines and quality standards.

☑ You've communicated *why* it matters.

When you explain purpose, people deliver excellence.

Maintaining Quality and Culture

Your business's soul is how clients feel when they work with you.

As you expand, protect that feeling.

Create a Culture of Clarity

Hold a brief weekly team check-in (even if it's just you + one contractor).

Agenda: wins, challenges, upcoming priorities.

Thirty minutes keeps everyone aligned and motivated.

Feedback Loops

Ask your team:

- "What's working well?"
- "Where are we losing time?"
- "What ideas do you have to improve client experience?"

They'll see problems you don't—and solutions you'd never think of.

Listening keeps morale high and innovation constant.

Embed Your Values Everywhere

If "care" is one of your brand words, teach it.

If "clarity" is your promise, model it.

Culture isn't slogans—it's repetition.

Write a short "Client Experience Code." Example:

1. Respond within 24 hours.
2. Communicate with kindness.
3. Always explain the why behind numbers.
4. Leave every interaction better than you found it.

Post it where your team sees it daily.

Story – Naomi's Standard

Naomi grew from solo to a five-person team.

To keep service consistent, she introduced "Friday Five": each Friday her team emailed her five highlights from the week—three client wins, one lesson learned, one suggestion.

It took ten minutes and became their rhythm of accountability and celebration.

Her retention rate hit 98 %.

Quality thrives in rhythm.

Scaling Services and Revenue

Expansion isn't just about more people; it's about deeper value.

Add Strategic Services

As experience grows, you can introduce higher-level offers:

- Cleanup Projects: high-ticket, time-limited jobs that create instant cash flow.

- Payroll Management: recurring revenue add-on.

- Advisory and Reporting: monthly strategy calls analyzing trends.

- Training Packages: teaching clients' staff basic bookkeeping for a fee.

Each layer serves existing clients better while increasing income per account.

Refine Pricing

Move from hourly to fixed or tiered packages.

Example:

- *Essential Package* – basic bookkeeping $500 / month

- *Growth Package* – bookkeeping + reports $850 / month

- *Executive Package* – full advisory $1 200 / month

Packages simplify sales and scale faster than tracking minutes.

Raise Rates with Confidence

If your demand outpaces capacity, prices are too low.

Notify clients respectfully:

"To continue providing the same level of service and attention, my rates will increase on [date]. I truly value our partnership and look forward to supporting your continued growth."

Most clients happily stay—because they trust you.

Diversify Income Streams

Think beyond direct service:

- Templates or mini-courses for DIY business owners.

- Affiliate partnerships with software you use.

- Consulting for other bookkeepers starting out.

Multiple streams create resilience and freedom.

Stories of Expansion

1. Grace – From Freelancer to Firm Owner

Grace started in her kitchen with two clients. After documenting everything and hiring a VA, she added a junior bookkeeper six months later.

Within two years she managed a small remote team of four and tripled income.

Her key? "I stopped trying to be the hero and became the conductor."

2. Leo – The Niche Specialist

Leo focused on contractors. He built SOPs tailored to that niche, created a custom onboarding video, and launched "Contractor Cash-Flow Coaching" as an add-on.

His referrals exploded because clients finally felt someone *understood their world.*

Niche + system = momentum.

3. Ana – The Freedom Builder

Ana vowed never to work weekends again.

She automated 80 % of admin tasks and trained her assistant to handle client updates.

Revenue climbed 40 %, hours dropped 30 %.

Her takeaway: "Scaling didn't mean more work; it meant smarter work."

Protecting Freedom While You Grow

Growth can quietly rebuild the cage you escaped—unless you protect freedom deliberately.

Redesign Your Schedule

Block CEO time weekly for strategy, learning, and rest.

Color-code your calendar:

- *Blue* = Client work
- *Green* = Growth tasks
- *Yellow* = Personal time

If you see no yellow, pause. You're building a business, not a burnout factory.

Delegate for Balance, Not Bragging Rights

Don't hire just to sound bigger. Hire to feel lighter.

Every role should buy you time for what only you can do: vision, leadership, relationships.

Guard Your Boundaries

Success attracts opportunities—and distractions.

Say yes to what aligns with your purpose; say no quickly to what doesn't.

Freedom thrives in focus.

Celebrate Milestones

Every system completed, every hire trained, every weekend off—that's a win.

Write them down. Gratitude anchors growth.

Transition to Chapter 8 – Maintaining Work-Life Harmony

You've built systems, trained support, and expanded your reach.

Now comes the art of sustaining it all without losing yourself.

In Chapter 8 – Maintaining Work-Life Harmony, we'll explore:

- How to manage success without slipping back into stress.

- Practical boundaries for long-term balance.

- The habits and rituals that keep your freedom intact.

Because scaling means nothing if you're too tired to enjoy the life it creates.

The next chapter ensures the business you've built continues to serve *you*—mind, body, and soul.

Additional resources, case studies, forms, and more are waiting for you at https://stayathomebookkeeper.co/resource. Visit the site now and enjoy a huge collection of resources that are absolutely free!

Chapter 8

Maintaining
Work-Life Harmony

Why Harmony Matters More Than Balance

People talk about *work-life balance* as if life were a seesaw—work on one side, family and freedom on the other.

But the truth is, balance is brittle. Tilt too far either way and something falls.

Harmony is different. Harmony is music. Each part—your work, your family, your health, your joy—plays at its own volume, in rhythm with the others.

Some days the "work" instrument will be loud; on others, the "life" section will take the solo.

When the song is yours, it can change tempo without losing tune.

You built this business for freedom. But freedom without harmony can quietly become another trap—busier than corporate, lonelier than a cubicle, heavier than any boss you ever had.

So this chapter is about keeping your freedom sustainable—protecting the peace you worked so hard to earn.

The Cost of Imbalance

At first, overworking feels noble. *Just one more client. Just one more report.*

Then the skipped workouts pile up, the family dinners get shorter, and weekends blur into spreadsheets.

You start feeling that old corporate fatigue again, only now you can't blame a manager—it's your name on the door.

Success without rest is still failure.

Because the real goal isn't income—it's impact, experienced joyfully and sustainably.

A Moment of Truth – Kelly's Wake-Up

Kelly's bookkeeping firm hit six figures by year two. She was proud—and permanently tired.

Her eight-year-old asked one night, "Mom, are you still at work?" while she typed at the dinner table.

That question landed like a stone.

The next morning she built a new rule: *No laptop after 6 p.m.*

It felt impossible for the first week. Then her evenings filled with laughter instead of ledgers.

Her energy doubled. So did her clarity.

Harmony starts with one brave boundary.

The Four Pillars of Sustainable Freedom

Freedom stands on four supports.

If any one cracks, the others wobble.

1. Health – Your Energy Engine

You are the engine of your business.

Without fuel, the vehicle stops.

Move daily—even ten-minute walks count.

Hydrate, stretch, rest. Schedule health the way you schedule clients.

Quick Habit: "Walk the Block Rule."

Between client sessions, step outside for five minutes. Sunlight resets your brain faster than coffee.

Eat real food. Sleep enough.

Remember: tired decisions are expensive decisions.

2. Relationships – Your Support System

Freedom means little if you experience it alone.

Protect time for the people who make you laugh, challenge you, and remind you you're more than an entrepreneur.

When you're present, be *fully* present.

Close the laptop. Face the person in front of you.

Mini Ritual: "Phone Down Dinners."

No screens. Just connection.

The ROI? Joy, grounding, perspective.

Your loved ones are part of this business—they fuel the purpose behind every goal.

3. Finances – Your Stability Anchor

Ironically, many bookkeepers neglect their own books.

Treat yourself like a VIP client.

Pay yourself first, budget intentionally, plan taxes early.

Separate "business growth money" from "peace money."

Growth money builds the future; peace money keeps anxiety silent today.

Run quarterly personal reviews: income, savings, generosity.

Harmony thrives when your numbers tell a calm story.

4. Purpose – Your Guiding North Star

Money and flexibility are wonderful, but purpose sustains you when excitement fades.

Ask yourself often:

- Who am I helping right now?

- Why does it matter?

- How does this align with the life I want to model?

Purpose gives your work meaning beyond invoices.

It turns fatigue into fulfillment.

Story – Derrick's Reset

Derrick almost quit after a grueling tax season. Then one client said, "Because of you, I finally paid myself this year."

That single sentence reignited him.

Purpose is fuel you can't buy.

Time Mastery, Not Time Management

Time management suggests squeezing more into the same 24 hours.

Time mastery means deciding *what belongs* in those hours at all.

Design Your Ideal Week

Instead of asking "How can I fit everything?" ask "What's worth fitting?"

Start by mapping your current week.

Then rebuild it around priorities that reflect your pillars.

Example:

Day	Focus	Notes
Monday	CEO planning	review metrics, set goals
Tuesday – Thursday	Client work	3 main blocks per day
Friday AM	Marketing & learning	creative tasks only
Friday PM	Admin & wrap-up	inbox zero, clear brain for weekend

Color-code tasks: blue = client, green = growth, yellow = personal.

If yellow disappears, rebalance.

Batch Your Energy

Group similar tasks together—emails in one block, reconciliations in another.

Every time you switch contexts, you lose focus.

Batching gives back hidden hours.

Use a timer or app like Pomodoro to keep sprints intentional: 50 minutes on, 10 off.

Guard Your Deep Work

Deep work is distraction-free focus on what matters most.

Bookkeepers need this for reconciliations, forecasting, and strategy.

Create rituals that protect it:

- Noise-canceling headphones.

- "Do Not Disturb" mode.

- Notify family: "From 9-11 a.m., I'm in flow."

Two focused hours can outperform six scattered ones.

Automate Your Time Decisions

We often waste mental energy deciding when to do things.

Automate decisions through routines.

Example:

- Mondays = planning.

- First Friday = billing.

- Second Tuesday = marketing.

Predictable rhythms prevent procrastination.

The Power of Boundaries

Every "yes" to something is a "no" to something else.

Protect time like profit—limited, precious, intentional.

When a client asks for a meeting outside hours, you can say:

"My calendar's full that evening, but I have Tuesday morning available."

That's professional, not rigid.

Boundaries teach clients how to treat you.

Micro-Habits That Multiply Time

1. Start-of-Day Intention (2 minutes): Write the top 3 results you want by sunset.

2. Mid-Day Reset (5 minutes): Step away, breathe, stretch.

3. End-of-Day Review (3 minutes): Note wins and tomorrow's first task.

Ten minutes daily compounds into hours of clarity each week.

Story – Lena's Calendar Comeback

Lena once let clients book her anytime. Her calendar looked like confetti.

She switched to Calendly with set availability—Tuesdays and Thursdays only for meetings.

Within two weeks her focus doubled and clients respected her time.

"When you train people how to access you, they appreciate you more," she says.

Boundaries don't push people away; they draw respect closer.

The Mental Game – Managing Pressure and Perfectionism

Freedom brings new pressure: no boss, no safety net, no one else to blame.

Left unchecked, that independence can morph into perfectionism—the illusion that every detail must be flawless to prove your worth.

But perfectionism is just fear dressed in productivity.

It whispers, *"If I get everything right, I'll finally feel safe."*

You already are safe. You built something that works. Now your job is to protect the person who built it.

Recognize Burnout Early

Burnout rarely explodes; it erodes.

Watch for the subtle signs:

- You wake up already tired.

- You avoid checking email because it triggers dread.

- You feel resentful of clients you once loved.

Those aren't signs of weakness—they're signals for rest.

When you notice them, take action within 48 hours. Step away for a walk, delegate a task, block a weekend off. Small rests prevent big crashes.

Shift From Pressure to Purpose

When the work feels heavy, reconnect to *why* you started.

Write it down again. Post it by your desk.

Purpose doesn't erase pressure—it puts it in perspective.

Story – Eva's Reset

Eva ran a thriving bookkeeping firm but felt trapped by constant comparison. "Everyone else seemed further ahead."

One Friday she turned off notifications, sat in silence, and wrote, *"My business exists to create peace for families—including mine."*

That sentence became her filter. She dropped two misaligned clients and gained back her sanity.

Mindset Tools

1. Reflection: End each week asking, "What energized me? What drained me?"

2. Gratitude: List three wins—no matter how small. Gratitude retrains your brain toward abundance.

3. Self-Compassion: When mistakes happen, speak to yourself like you'd speak to a client you adore—kindly, constructively, never cruelly.

Integrating Family and Flexibility

Work from home doesn't automatically mean harmony—it means boundaries need to move *inside* the house too.

Include Loved Ones in the Vision

Explain your business goals to your family.

Say:

"This isn't just my work—it's what allows us more freedom together. Here's how you can help me protect it."

When family understands the purpose behind your schedule, they become allies instead of interruptions.

Create Visible Signals

Simple cues keep home and work in rhythm:

- Door open = available. Door closed = focus time.

- Headphones on = deep work.

- Family calendar shared digitally so everyone sees commitments.

Small structure prevents big friction.

Plan Joy on Purpose

Don't wait for "someday" to enjoy flexibility.

Take a mid-day walk with your partner.

Schedule a Tuesday picnic because you can.

Freedom unused turns stale; use it.

Story – The River Rule

The Reyes family runs their bookkeeping business near a river in Montana.

Every Friday at 3 p.m., no matter how busy, they walk the trail together.

They call it "The River Rule."

"Clients can wait an hour," they say. "Our kids' memories can't."

Harmony is built by traditions like that—small, sacred, scheduled joy.

Stories of Balance Restored

Mark's 180-Degree Turn

Mark prided himself on responsiveness. His phone dinged 24/7.

One night his spouse asked, "Are we part of your notifications too?"

He deleted Slack from his phone, set auto-responses, and promised replies within business hours.

A week later he was sleeping through the night again—and productivity rose.

Boundaries aren't walls; they're windows that let light back in.

Nora's Mini-Sabbatical

After three intense years, Nora felt detached from her own business. She scheduled a two-week "working sabbatical": mornings for reflection, afternoons for hobbies.

During that break, she realized her true passion was mentoring other bookkeepers.

She returned refreshed, launched a coaching offer, and doubled income doing work she loved.

Rest doesn't pause growth—it reveals direction.

Rituals of Renewal

Freedom fades without renewal.

Build rhythms that refill your energy before it empties.

Morning Reset

- Wake slowly—no phone for the first 30 minutes.

- Read, pray, or journal one page of intention.

- Move your body.

- Ask: "What does success look like *today*?" (Not this month, not this year—today.)

Evening Wind-Down

- Review wins, not worries.

- Write tomorrow's top 3 priorities so your mind can rest.

- End with gratitude or a quick reflection: *"I'm proud that I…"*

Weekly Recharge

Pick one half-day each week with no screens.

Hike, paint, garden, nap—anything that restores rather than produces.

The work will wait; the moment won't.

Digital Detox

Try "Screen-Free Sundays."

Silence notifications, unplug devices, and remember what quiet sounds like.

You'll return Monday sharper than any all-nighter could make you.

Mini-Sabbaticals

Every six months, schedule a week to *not* schedule.

Even if you stay home, disconnect from business.

Your creativity will thank you.

Looking Ahead – The Freedom Legacy

Work-life harmony isn't a finish line; it's a living practice.

It's the art of protecting peace as fiercely as profit.

You began this journey chasing freedom—time, money, purpose.

Now you understand that freedom multiplies only when you care for the one who built it.

Your Legacy Isn't What You Earn—It's What You Model

Your children, friends, and clients are watching how you work.

When they see you rest without guilt, say no with grace, and live aligned with values, you give them permission to do the same.

You become proof that success and serenity can coexist.

A Final Story – The Campfire

On a cool evening in Texas, DeAnna and her husband closed their laptops early.

They sat by the fire with their kids, roasting marshmallows.

The stars were bright, and the phones were off.

He looked over and said, "Remember when we thought working for ourselves would be the hard part?"

She laughed. "Turns out, the real work was learning to stop working."

That's the essence of harmony: knowing when enough is enough—and feeling grateful in that enoughness.

Transition to the Closing Chapter

You've learned how to build, brand, scale, and sustain a business that serves your life.

The final chapter will bring it all together—your personal *Freedom Blueprint*: how to keep growing, keep giving, and keep living fully on your terms.

Because bookkeeping was never just about numbers.

It was about reclaiming your rhythm—and guarding the life you were meant to enjoy.

Additional resources, case studies, forms, and more are waiting for you at https://stayathomebookkeeper.co/resource. Visit the site now and enjoy a huge collection of resources that are absolutely free!

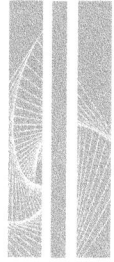

Chapter 9

The Shortcut: Leveraging the Stay at Home Bookkeeper Academy

Stay at Home
BOOKKEEPER ACADEMY

The Power of Guidance

Every great success story has a guide.

Athletes have coaches. Musicians have mentors. Pilots have copilots.

Even the best entrepreneurs—those we admire for their confidence and vision—built their empires with people who'd already walked the path.

Building a bookkeeping business is no different. You can go alone, but you don't have to.

When you're trying to grow something new, you don't just need information—you need *interpretation*. You need someone to say, "Do this next. Skip that for now. Here's how to stay out of the ditch."

That's what mentorship does. It turns confusion into clarity and turns your learning curve into a straight line.

When you joined this book, you started with curiosity. You've now learned the foundations—mindset, branding, systems, relationships.

But reading alone can only take you so far. Execution requires accountability. That's where *The Stay at Home Bookkeeper Academy* becomes the game-changer.

The Shortcut vs. the Slow Road

Let's be honest—there are two ways to build a business:

1. The Slow Road

You try to piece everything together yourself.

You watch hundreds of videos, download free PDFs, and second-guess every move.

You start, stop, start again.

You spend more time researching than reaching clients.

It's exhausting—and expensive in invisible ways: lost time, lost momentum, lost confidence.

2. The Shortcut

You follow a proven path with people who've already done it.

You plug into a community that answers questions in minutes instead of months.

You receive structure, scripts, and support so you can move from idea to income quickly—and sustainably.

That's the Shortcut.

It's not cheating. It's choosing efficiency.

Because time is your most limited currency. Every week you wait to act is a week your freedom sits on hold.

Inside the Stay at Home Bookkeeper Academy

The Academy was built for people exactly like you—smart, capable, and ready to turn skill into freedom.

It's the roadmap thousands have used to start, grow, and scale bookkeeping businesses from home.

Let's take a guided tour so you know what's inside and how it helps.

1. Step-by-Step Training

The curriculum is designed to meet you where you are, whether you're brand-new to bookkeeping or returning with experience.

It's laid out in clear, digestible modules:

- **Module 1 – Mindset & Vision:** Clarify your goals, define success, and set up the routines that keep you grounded.

- **Module 2 – Bookkeeping Basics:** Master QuickBooks Online, transactions, reconciliations, and client workflows.

- **Module 3 – Business Setup:** Choose your structure, open your accounts, create contracts, and set prices.

- **Module 4 – Brand & Marketing:** Everything from naming your business to building social presence and client-getting strategies.

- **Module 5 – Client Management:** Onboarding, communication, retention, and how to deliver five-star service.

- **Module 6 – Scaling & Freedom:** Systems, automation, and hiring so you can expand without burning out.

Each module ends with checklists and templates so you can implement immediately instead of wondering "what now?"

2. Live Coaching and Q&A Calls

Information alone isn't enough; feedback creates mastery.

The Academy offers live weekly calls with experienced bookkeepers and mentors.

Bring real questions, get real answers.

You're not a username—you're part of a conversation.

3. Templates & Tools

Inside the portal you'll find:

- Client proposals and engagement letters.

- Pricing calculators.

- Email and discovery-call scripts.

- Marketing swipe files.

- SOP templates for onboarding and monthly workflows.

These aren't theory—they're the same resources top earners use daily. Plug them in and go.

4. Community of Encouragement

The private Academy community is where breakthroughs happen.

It's not a place for comparison; it's a place for collaboration.

Students share wins, troubleshoot issues, and celebrate together.

You'll find yourself surrounded by people who understand what you're building—because they're building it too.

One post away from advice. One call away from clarity.

You're never alone again.

The Academy Framework

The Academy isn't random lessons—it's a progression, a *success path*.

Each phase builds confidence, competence, and cash flow.

Phase 1 – Start

You'll set up your foundation.

- ✅ Choose a business name.
- ✅ Open your bank account and get your EIN.
- ✅ Learn the basics of QuickBooks Online.
- ✅ Create your first brand presence.
- ✅ Draft your first simple offer.

Goal: move from "idea" to "I have a real business."

Phase 2 – Build

Here you move from setup to service.

- [x] Find and onboard your first paying client using proven scripts.
- [x] Establish your workflow and reporting process.
- [x] Learn to manage time and boundaries.

Goal: earn consistent monthly income while refining your systems.

Phase 3 – Grow

Now you focus on leverage.

- [x] Streamline with automation.
- [x] Increase pricing confidently.
- [x] Add value through advisory and cleanup projects.
- [x] Learn soft-skills that turn clients into advocates.

Goal: work fewer hours while earning more.

Phase 4 – Scale

Here, freedom truly expands.

- [x] Document processes.
- [x] Hire help strategically.
- [x] Build a small team or agency if you choose.
- [x] Add multiple income streams (courses, consulting, affiliate partnerships).

Goal: a sustainable business that serves your life—not the other way around.

Why This Framework Works

Because it's not just theory—it's lived experience from people who've walked the same journey.

Each stage includes milestones so you always know exactly where you are and what comes next.

No more wandering. No more wasted energy.

The Academy collapses months of trial and error into a clear, step-by-step path backed by mentorship and community.

Mentorship in Motion

Knowledge is potential power.

Mentorship is what turns it into motion.

Inside The Stay at Home Bookkeeper Academy, you're not just learning from lessons—you're learning from leaders. Every mentor has built their own thriving bookkeeping business, and they've faced the same doubts, detours, and growing pains that you're experiencing now.

They know what it feels like to stare at your laptop wondering, *"What do I do next?"*

They've been through that fear of sending the first proposal, that awkwardness of quoting a price, that thrill of getting the first "Yes!"

Weekly Coaching Calls

Each week, live coaching calls are held where you can bring your real questions—about software, clients, mindset, pricing, anything—and get practical, tested answers.

You'll hear stories, strategies, and encouragement from mentors who blend heart and strategy.

One student once said, "It's like having a whole advisory board cheering for me every week."

And it's true—these calls don't just teach; they *transfer courage.*

Accountability That Works

Left alone, we all drift.

A mentor's role is to keep you focused on the *right* next step.

They hold you accountable to the goals you set—not by pressure, but by presence.

Each month, you'll be guided to set clear targets:

- "How many outreach messages will I send?"

- "What client conversations am I scheduling?"

- "Which system am I refining?"

Progress isn't random anymore; it's measured. And momentum becomes your new normal.

Mentorship shortens the distance between "thinking about it" and "living it."

Community Over Competition

Entrepreneurship can be lonely—unless you're surrounded by people who get it.

Inside the Academy, competition simply doesn't exist. Instead, collaboration thrives.

Students share scripts, celebrate wins, and encourage each other through challenges. You'll find threads where someone posts, *"Just signed my first $1,000 client!"* and within minutes, fifty others cheer.

There's power in belonging.

When you share space with people building businesses like yours, your standard rises. You stop asking, *"Can I do this?"* and start asking, *"How fast can I do this?"*

The Power of Shared Success

Imagine a community where advice flows freely and generosity replaces scarcity.

You'll see advanced students mentoring newcomers, moms balancing family life while onboarding clients, retirees rediscovering purpose.

This diversity makes the community dynamic, supportive, and deeply human.

Every win, no matter how small, becomes fuel for the next person's breakthrough.

Stories of Transformation

Let's bring it to life. These are real patterns repeated again and again inside the Academy—people from every walk of life who followed the framework and found freedom.

1. Crystal – The Confident Beginner

Crystal joined the Academy with zero business experience. She'd been out of the workforce for ten years raising her kids and wasn't sure she had anything valuable to offer.

In her first coaching call, her mentor helped her write her brand story and craft a simple, clear message. Within three weeks, she had her first discovery call.

That client became her first $700/month retainer.

A year later, Crystal had ten clients and her husband said, "You've built something real."

Her words now? *"The Academy gave me the courage to start before I felt ready—and the tools to succeed once I did."*

2. James – The Burned-Out Accountant

James had worked in corporate accounting for fifteen years. The hours were relentless, and his creativity was buried under red tape.

He joined the Academy skeptical, thinking, *"Can I really replace my salary from home?"*

Within four months, he did.

Using the Academy's growth scripts, he built a client base of local business owners who wanted personalized attention. He now makes more, works less, and coaches new students part-time inside the program.

"The system works," he says. "But it's the people that change you."

3. Alana – The Empty-Nest Dreamer

Alana was 52 when she joined. Her kids were grown, and she wanted something meaningful that would also provide income for travel.

She followed the Academy's Start → Build → Grow pathway, focused on boutique clients she enjoyed working with, and within six months she had a thriving roster.

Her testimonial said it best: *"I thought I was too old to start over. Turns out, I was just in time."*

Patterns You'll Notice

Each story is different, yet the rhythm is the same:

1. They decided.

2. They plugged into structure.

3. They followed mentorship.

4. They found freedom.

The Academy doesn't create your success; it *accelerates* what you already have inside you.

Your Guided Path Forward

You've come this far—reading, reflecting, learning, dreaming.

Now it's time to step into guided action.

Step 1 – Commit to the Shortcut

You can keep trying to piece things together on your own, or you can compress years of trial and error into months of growth.

The Stay at Home Bookkeeper Academy exists to help you do just that.

It's not about luck—it's about leadership. Your leadership.

Step 2 – Plug Into Support

Once you join, you'll immediately receive access to:

- The full course curriculum (the same structure outlined earlier).

- Weekly live coaching calls with multiple mentors.

- A private, supportive community of thousands of members.

- Templates, scripts, and resources ready to use day one.

Within the first week, you'll know exactly where to start and who to reach out to for help.

No more spinning wheels. No more overwhelm.

Step 3 – Take Your First 90 Days Seriously

The first 90 days inside the Academy are designed for momentum.

You'll:

☑ Launch your business foundation (brand, systems, outreach).

☑ Land your first client or practice account.

☑ Develop your daily rhythm for success.

You'll also participate in milestone celebrations and accountability challenges that make progress fun.

Within three months, most students can say, "I'm not guessing anymore. I'm growing."

Step 4 – Stay Connected

The Academy doesn't end after you complete modules—it evolves with you.

As your business grows, you'll gain access to advanced training on scaling, hiring, and automation.

You'll meet peers who become collaborators and mentors who become friends.

This isn't a course. It's a *continuing community of freedom-builders.*

Why This Shortcut Works

Because it combines the three things every entrepreneur needs but rarely finds together:

1. Clarity – A proven path.

2. Community – People walking beside you.

3. Confidence – Mentorship that reminds you what's possible.

When you join, you don't just get tools—you get *transferable belief.*

Belief that you can do this.

Belief that you're capable of more.

Belief that the life you pictured when you started reading this book is waiting on the other side of action.

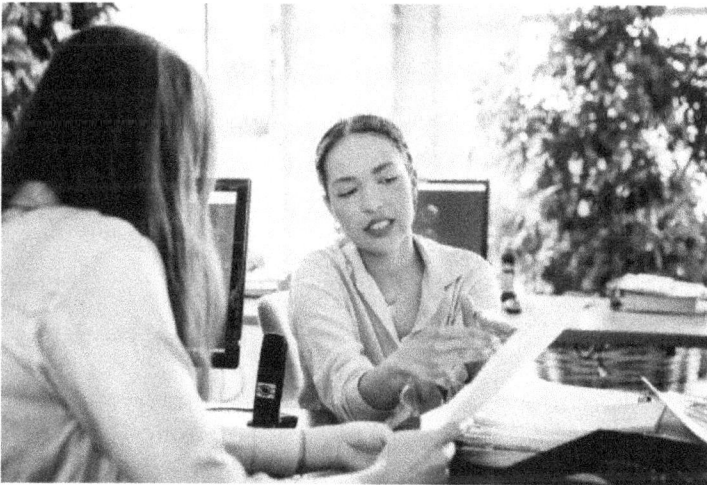

Your Invitation

You've spent these chapters building vision, systems, and self-belief.

Now, the shortcut is simple: stop building alone.

The Stay at Home Bookkeeper Academy was created so you can succeed faster, with less stress, and more joy.

It's your bridge between what you know and what you're meant to live.

If you're ready to:

- Build your business the right way.

- Create consistent income from home.

- Be surrounded by mentors who care about your success.

- And finally live *life on your terms*—

Then the next step is waiting for you.

Visit **StayAtHomeBookkeeper.com** to learn more, connect with the team, or join the next cohort of entrepreneurs rewriting their stories.

Because the real shortcut isn't just a program—it's a decision.

A decision to believe that your freedom can start today.

Transition to Chapter 10 – Your Freedom Blueprint

In the final chapter, we'll tie it all together—the mindset, systems, relationships, and support that form your personal *Freedom Blueprint*.

You'll see how to protect what you've built, scale it gracefully, and continue growing into the person you were always meant to be.

Because bookkeeping was never just about numbers—it was about creating a life that adds up beautifully.

Additional resources, case studies, forms, and more are waiting for you at https://stayathomebookkeeper.co/resource. Visit the site now and enjoy a huge collection of resources that are absolutely free!

Chapter 10

Your Freedom Blueprint

The Journey So Far

Take a moment to breathe.

Think about where you started when you first opened this book.

Maybe you were stuck in a job that no longer fit.

Maybe you were searching for flexibility, purpose, or proof that you could build something of your own.

You might have been curious, skeptical, or hopeful—but you were ready.

Page by page, you've walked the journey of transformation.

You learned how to think like an entrepreneur, create a brand with confidence, build systems that scale, and nurture relationships that last.

You discovered that freedom isn't a fantasy—it's a framework.

And you've learned that the key to lasting success isn't doing everything yourself; it's finding the right support, community, and rhythm to keep growing.

Every story in these chapters began just like yours—with a person who decided to take one small step forward.

Some of them did it through trial and error.

Most of them found their way faster through mentorship and guidance.

That's why *The Stay at Home Bookkeeper Academy* exists—to be that bridge between desire and direction, between learning and living.

You've already proven you can do this.

Now it's about keeping that momentum and turning knowledge into daily practice.

That's what this final chapter is for.

Your *Freedom Blueprint* is the map that keeps your business steady, your mindset strong, and your lifestyle aligned with what matters most.

The Freedom Blueprint Framework

Freedom doesn't happen by accident. It's designed through intention.

Every successful bookkeeper who's built a thriving business from home follows a pattern—five essential pillars that keep their success balanced and sustainable.

Think of these as the core structure of your ongoing journey.

1. Mindset – The Foundation of Belief

Every result begins with a thought.

When you believe that you can create stability and freedom through your skills, your actions naturally align with that belief.

Doubt still shows up, but it no longer drives.

Keep returning to the mindset tools you've built: daily gratitude, purpose-driven reflection, and self-compassion.

Remember that you're not running a bookkeeping business—you're leading a life by design.

Inside the Academy, mindset remains central because entrepreneurs never stop battling limiting beliefs.

Every level of success brings new challenges, and the community helps you navigate each one with perspective.

2. Model – The Structure That Supports You

A business without structure is a hobby that pays inconsistently.

You've already learned how to design your model: systems, services, and pricing that match your goals.

Your model defines how you operate—what you offer, who you serve, and how you deliver results.

The clearer your model, the easier every decision becomes.

Review it every quarter. Ask:

- Does this still fit my life?

- Do these services still align with my strengths?

- Am I charging what I'm worth?

If something feels heavy, refine it.

You're allowed to rebuild. That's the beauty of ownership.

One of the reasons the Academy's program works so well is that it gives students a tested model to start from—no guesswork, no wasted motion.

Once you master the structure, you can make it your own.

3. Mechanics – The Tools and Systems

This is where freedom becomes tangible.

Mechanics are the workflows, software, and automations that keep your business running without constant attention.

You've seen how systems protect your sanity: client onboarding checklists, templates for communication, automations that eliminate repetition.

These mechanics make your business scalable—and they make your time valuable.

The more efficient your systems, the more energy you free up for strategy, creativity, and life.

Inside the Academy, you'll find plug-and-play templates, walkthroughs, and community feedback on every major tool—from QuickBooks setups to client management automations—so you can skip the trial phase and move straight to execution.

4. Mentorship – The Acceleration Factor

No one succeeds alone.

Mentorship collapses years into months.

It provides perspective when you're too close to the problem and accountability when you're tempted to drift.

When you surround yourself with mentors who have achieved what you want, you borrow their clarity until it becomes your own.

This is what makes the Stay at Home Bookkeeper Academy such a unique force—it's not a course, it's a coaching ecosystem.

Mentors aren't distant experts; they're practitioners who remember what starting felt like.

They've built what you're building.

They'll remind you of your potential on the days you forget.

Keep this principle with you even beyond the Academy: success always accelerates with guidance.

5. Maintenance – The Long Game

Freedom must be maintained or it quietly fades back into chaos.

Maintenance means protecting what you've built through consistent review, healthy routines, and reflection.

Check your systems quarterly, your finances monthly, and your mindset daily.

This is where your habits sustain your results.

The most successful bookkeepers inside the Academy are not the ones who sprint—they're the ones who maintain momentum steadily. They show up, apply feedback, refine, and keep growing.

Your goal isn't perfection—it's persistence.

Building Momentum After the Book

You've reached the end of the written roadmap, but your real journey is just beginning.

This next phase is about implementing what you know—and doing it with intention.

The following 90-day blueprint will help you turn everything you've learned into measurable progress.

The 90-Day Freedom Plan

Month 1 – Foundation and Focus

- Review your business structure: pricing, offers, and client list.

- Eliminate one inefficiency that's stealing time.

- Create or refine your morning and evening routines.

- Identify your "why" again and write it where you'll see it daily.

Month 2 – Connection and Consistency

- Reach out to five potential clients or referral partners.

- Post twice per week on one platform consistently.

- Improve one system with automation or delegation.

- Schedule one personal day for pure rest and creativity.

Month 3 – Refinement and Growth

- Review financial goals and progress.

- Celebrate milestones.

- Document what worked and what didn't.

- Plan your next quarter using those insights.

If you thrive on accountability and prefer to grow within a structured environment, the Academy is built to walk you through exactly this kind of rhythm—step by step, with community support that keeps you on track.

Because real freedom doesn't come from doing more.

It comes from doing what matters—with guidance and intention.

Sustaining the Lifestyle You Created

You've built something extraordinary—a business that gives you choices.

Now the challenge shifts from creation to preservation.

Freedom, once earned, must be protected with as much care as it was built.

The Habits That Hold It Together

The entrepreneurs who stay free share certain rhythms.

They:

- Plan each week on purpose. Monday mornings aren't surprises; they're strategy sessions.

- Review, don't react. They look at reports before they look at emails.

- Protect their energy. If a task drains them repeatedly, they automate, delegate, or delete it.

- Keep learning. Even seasoned business owners join trainings, read books, and surround themselves with mentors.

Success is not a one-time decision. It's a daily discipline of alignment.

That's why the Academy never stops at helping you start. It continues to provide new tools, updated resources, and coaching so your business grows *with* you instead of outgrowing you.

When to Scale, When to Simplify

Freedom doesn't always mean expansion. Sometimes it means editing.

Every six months, ask:

- Do my clients still align with my values?

- Is this system helping or complicating my workflow?

- What can I stop doing without hurting results?

Growth is healthy only when it stays congruent with your life.

Simplify whenever success starts to feel heavy.

You built this business to support your lifestyle, not to smother it.

Legacy Thinking

At this point, you're not just running a bookkeeping business. You're shaping a legacy.

Your business is proof that independence is possible—especially for people who once believed it wasn't.

You're showing your children, peers, and community what's achievable when courage meets consistency.

Legacy isn't a logo or a balance sheet; it's the ripple of inspiration you leave behind.

Every client you help, every student you mentor, every person you encourage to follow their dream adds to that ripple.

Stories of Continuation

Case Study 1 – Emma's Evolution

Emma started her bookkeeping business while her youngest child was still in preschool. At first, she worked during nap times, completing reconciliations at the kitchen table.

Within a year, she had five clients. Within two, she had a team.

But more importantly, she had time.

Every Thursday afternoon, she blocks her calendar for "Mom dates"— bike rides, ice cream, laughter.

She often says, "Bookkeeping gave me money. The Academy taught me how to buy my time back."

Case Study 2 – Victor's Vision

Victor joined the Academy after twenty years in a corporate accounting department. He'd forgotten what creativity felt like.

He built his client base around small family-owned restaurants, combining his analytical skills with his love for food service.

Now, he mentors other members inside the Academy, reminding them, "You're not just balancing books. You're building freedom for people who feed communities."

Victor's story shows that fulfillment multiplies when you give back to the next generation of entrepreneurs.

Case Study 3 – Tasha's Transformation

Tasha was nearing retirement when she decided to start her own business. She worried it was too late.

Her mentor told her, "It's never too late to design the next chapter."

Two years later, Tasha runs a boutique bookkeeping practice for wellness coaches.

She takes Fridays off, travels with her husband, and jokes, "Retirement didn't give me freedom—ownership did."

Her story is now shared with new students who need to see what's possible when belief and structure meet.

Final Encouragement: The Freedom Mindset

If there's one lesson this book—and this journey—has taught you, it's that freedom isn't something you wait for. It's something you build, moment by moment, decision by decision.

It's built in the early mornings when you choose progress over perfection.

It's built in the boundaries you hold and the systems you design.

It's built every time you replace fear with focus and isolation with mentorship.

You've proven that you're capable of creating change.

Now the blueprint is yours:

- Mindset keeps you grounded.

- Model gives you structure.

- Mechanics make it run.

- Mentorship keeps you sharp.

- Maintenance sustains your success.

Keep refining. Keep showing up. Keep building a business that supports your best life.

And remember, you never have to walk the next stage alone.

The same mentorship and community that helped you find this freedom—*The Stay at Home Bookkeeper Academy*—will always be there to guide, inspire, and celebrate with you as you continue to grow.

A Letter from Us to You

You've reached the end of this book, but not the end of your story.

If you take nothing else from these pages, take this: your future is not determined by where you started; it's defined by what you decide next.

The life you want is closer than you think.

The tools are here, the pathway exists, and the support is waiting.

We've watched thousands of people step out of fear, out of fatigue, and into freedom through this journey. We know what happens when belief turns into action—it changes everything.

So take the next step.

Build boldly.

Protect your peace.

Lead your life on your terms.

And when you're ready to go further, your community—the Stay at Home Bookkeeper Academy—is ready to walk beside you.

You've got this.

Now go build something beautiful.

Bill and DeAnna

Additional resources, case studies, forms, and more are waiting for you at https://stayathomebookkeeper.co/resource. Visit the site now and enjoy a huge collection of resources that are absolutely free!

About the Authors

Bill Rogers

Bill Rogers is the Co-Founder and Owner of Rogers Capital Investments, North Star Automotive, Empower Growth Academy, and Evolve Events, and The Stay at Home Bookkeeper Academy.

A seasoned entrepreneur, investor, and mentor, Bill has built a career around empowering ordinary people to create extraordinary success through business ownership. After leaving a high-level corporate career in sales leadership and operations, Bill shifted his focus to helping others break free from traditional employment, gain financial control, and design lives they love.

Through his companies and coaching programs, Bill teaches practical frameworks for building wealth through entrepreneurship, consulting for equity, and small business acquisitions. He's known for transforming complex business concepts into simple, actionable strategies that anyone can follow—especially those starting from scratch or pivoting from the corporate world.

Bill's approach to mentorship is hands-on and rooted in real experience. He's passionate about showing people that they don't need an MBA, investors, or massive risk to own a thriving business. His work inside Empower Growth Academy and The Stay at Home Bookkeeper Academy has helped thousands of aspiring entrepreneurs—many with no prior business experience—replace their 9-to-5 income and gain the confidence to run successful, flexible, home-based businesses.

Driven by his belief that entrepreneurship is the greatest path to personal freedom, Bill continues to build, acquire, and grow companies that empower others to do the same. His message is simple but powerful: you don't have to start from nothing—you just have to start.

DeAnna Rogers

DeAnna Rogers is the Co-Founder and Owner of Rogers Capital Investments, Evolve Events, North Star Automotive, and Empower Growth Academy and The Stay at Home Bookkeeper Academy.

DeAnna is a nationally recognized entrepreneur, mentor, and strategist who has spent more than two decades helping people turn their passions into profitable, purpose-driven businesses. Known for her blend of heart, hustle, and strategy, she has built and scaled multiple 7- and 8-figure brands while guiding others to create freedom-based businesses that support their families and fulfill their purpose.

Her journey hasn't been without challenges. Overcoming personal adversity—including a battle with cancer—gave DeAnna a renewed mission: to help others reclaim their time, confidence, and financial independence. Through her companies, she teaches aspiring entrepreneurs, especially women, how to use bookkeeping and other service-based business models to build real, sustainable income from home.

As a driving force behind Empower Growth Academy and The Stay at Home Bookkeeper Academy, DeAnna has coached and inspired thousands of students to step into entrepreneurship with courage and clarity. Her leadership extends into EPIC Network, where she mentors business owners on advanced growth strategies, partnerships, and acquisitions.

Through Evolve Events, DeAnna creates powerful in-person experiences that bring communities together to learn, connect, and grow. Her mission is deeply personal—to help people believe in themselves, take action even when it's scary, and realize that they can build a business that truly supports the life they want.

DeAnna's message to every aspiring business owner is clear: you already have everything you need inside you; it's just time to believe it and take the next step.

www.ingramcontent.com/pod-product-compliance
Lightning Source LLC
Chambersburg PA
CBHW061725020426
42331CB00006B/1099